Linux Basics for SysAdmin

Learn core linux concepts and command-line skills to kickstart your system administration career

Ryan Juan

Published by: GitforGits

Publisher: Sonal Dhandre

www.gitforgits.com

support@gitforgits.com

Printed in India

First Printing: May 2024

ISBN: 9788119177561

Cover Design by: Kitten Publishing

Prologue

You have arrived at "Linux Basics for SysAdmin," a book that will teach you the ropes of Linux so that you may confidently administer Linux systems. Whether you're an experienced IT professional looking to hone your skills, a student eager to learn Linux, or someone in between, this book will cover all you need to know to become a competent system administrator.

A large number of computers, desktops, and mobile devices throughout the globe run Linux because of its flexibility and power. It is a priceless asset to the IT sector due to its open-source nature, robustness, and adaptability. Understanding the fundamental concepts that make Linux systems secure, efficient, and dependable is more important than simply knowing commands and configurations if you want to become an expert Linux user.

Beginning with the fundamentals, this book will provide you with the groundwork you need to become proficient with Linux. "Up and Running with Linux Systems," the first chapter, provides an overview of the Linux environment. A fundamental understanding of the shell, file and directory management, and command syntax will be covered. We also go over the basics of system starting and shutdown, managing packages, and the utilities that are needed for Linux administration.

Next, in Chapter 2, "Managing Linux Systems," we will explore system management in more detail. Discover the ins and outs of configuration files, learn how to use systemd to control services, crontab to schedule activities, and monitor system performance. Partitioning disks, managing log files, and SSH-based remote administration are all covered in this chapter.

When it comes to managing software and hardware, Chapter 3 is where it's at. This chapter will teach you the ins and outs of using apt and yum for package management, dealing with dependencies, configuring your system's hardware, and upgrading the kernel. Docker and VirtualBox, two popular tools for creating and managing virtual machines, are also covered in this chapter.

Chapter 4, "User and Permission Management," discusses how to manage users and permissions. Access Control Lists (ACLs), file ownership and permission settings, user profile editing, and account creation and management are all part of what you can expect. You will also be responsible for managing group memberships, working with Pluggable Authentication Modules (PAM), implementing password restrictions, configuring sudo, and user sessions.

This book will provide you the core concepts of Linux system administration practically, so you can start managing your systems with confidence. Starting here will go you far in the IT career path you desire by making you an expert Linux system administrator.

Content

Preface

For students, aspiring IT specialists, and working professionals, "Linux Basics for SysAdmin" is a great starting point for learning the fundamentals of Linux, including the command line and all the tools and commands needed to manage enterprise systems.

At first, you are introduced to the Linux environment, with a focus on browsing the filesystem, using basic commands, managing files and directories, and becoming acquainted with the shell. You'll also learn about package management and how to handle system startup and shutdown efficiently.

After that, you'll learn all about system configuration files, 'systemd' for managing system services, crontab for job scheduling, and 'at' and 'batch' for automating processes. You will also learn about system performance monitoring, log files, backup and restore procedures, disk partitioning, and remote management via SSH.

Afterwards, the book delves into topics such as dependency management, system hardware configuration, kernel upgrades, and device driver management, as well as package management with 'apt' and 'yum'. You'll also learn how to create and manage repositories, and install and setup virtual machines with VirtualBox. In the end, the book covers a wide range of topics, including creating and managing user accounts, editing user profiles, setting ownership and permissions for files, using ACLs, managing user sessions, configuring sudo for administrative tasks, implementing password policies, working with PAM, and managing group memberships.

In this book you will learn how to:

- Master essential Linux commands to efficiently navigate and manage the system's file structure.
- Gain proficiency in user and group management to ensure secure access control and permissions.
- Learn to configure and manage system services with systemd for streamlined service administration.
- Implement and enforce robust password policies for enhanced security and user account protection.
- Understand and utilize package management tools for seamless software installation.
- Set up and manage virtual machines with VirtualBox to create isolated, reproducible development environments.

- Use Access Control Lists (ACLs) to fine-tune file permissions beyond the standard Unix model.
- Schedule and automate tasks using cron, at, and batch to improve system efficiency and reliability.
- Monitor system performance and logs to proactively identify and address potential issues.
- Securely configure and use SSH for remote management and administration of Linux systems.

An understanding of the basics of Linux system administration will be yours by the time you finish this book.

Also, there is a companion book called "Linux Advanced for SysAdmin" for anyone who want to learn more advanced Linux techniques, by the same Author 'Ryan Juan'. Concepts like advanced database management, security configuration, network management, system monitoring, and advanced operations including deployments, load balancing, and working with Kubernetes are the main focus of this follow-up book. Each of these books, taken together, provide a solid foundation and advanced expertise for both aspiring and practicing Linux system administrators.

GitforGits

Prerequisites

This book is designed for IT professionals, aspiring system administrators, and students who want to acquire essential Linux skills. It is also suitable for any individual looking to build a strong foundation in Linux to advance their IT career.

Codes Usage

Are you in need of some helpful code examples to assist you in your programming and documentation? Look no further! Our book offers a wealth of supplemental material, including code examples and exercises.

Not only is this book here to aid you in getting your job done, but you have our permission to use the example code in your programs and documentation. However, please note that if you are reproducing a significant portion of the code, we do require you to contact us for permission.

But don't worry, using several chunks of code from this book in your program or answering a question by citing our book and quoting example code does not require permission. But if you do choose to give credit, an attribution typically includes the title, author, publisher, and ISBN. For example, "Linux Basics for SysAdmin by Ryan Juan".

If you are unsure whether your intended use of the code examples falls under fair use or the permissions outlined above, please do not hesitate to reach out to us at support@gitforgits.com.

We are happy to assist and clarify any concerns.

Acknowledgement

I owe a tremendous debt of gratitude to GitforGits, for their unflagging enthusiasm and wise counsel throughout the entire process of writing this book. Their knowledge and careful editing helped make sure the piece was useful for people of all reading levels and comprehension skills. In addition, I'd like to thank everyone involved in the publishing process for their efforts in making this book a reality. Their efforts, from copyediting to advertising, made the project what it is today.

Finally, I'd like to express my gratitude to everyone who has shown me unconditional love and encouragement throughout my life. Their support was crucial to the completion of this book. I appreciate your help with this endeavour and your continued interest in my career.

CHAPTER I: UP AND RUNNING WITH LINUX SYSTEMS

Overview

This chapter will set you on the path to becoming an expert Linux user, with an emphasis on the widely used Ubuntu distribution. Ubuntu is a popular operating system, and you will first learn what makes it special. Once you get the hang of managing directories and files in Linux, navigating the filesystem will be as natural as breathing. We will go over the most fundamental Linux commands so you can do basic activities quickly and easily. Get ready to dive into directory and file management like a pro! You'll learn how to effortlessly create, transfer, and remove files. In this chapter, you will also learn how to use the vi text editor, a powerful tool for editing files, and the shell, an interface for dealing with the system.

Another important topic you'll cover is package management, which involves installing, updating, and removing software packages to ensure your system is always up-to-date and runs properly. For proper management of your machine's boot sequence and power down, familiarity with the system's startup and shutdown procedures is vital. In order to keep tabs on and manage all of your system's applications, one of the most important skills you'll learn is process management. At last, you'll learn the ins and outs of Linux's utilities, which are robust programs that boost efficiency and let you do complicated jobs with just a few commands. The goal of this chapter is to provide you with a strong grounding in Linux so that you can manage common chores and become ready for more sophisticated system administration subjects.

Understanding Linux Ubuntu

Ubuntu, a popular and user-friendly Linux distribution, is renowned for its ease of use and robust community support. Developed by Canonical, Ubuntu is based on Debian and follows a regular release cycle, offering both Long Term Support (LTS) versions and interim releases. LTS versions, supported for five years, provide stability and extended support, making them ideal for production environments. Interim releases, with nine months of support, offer the latest features and improvements for those who want to stay on the cutting edge.

One of the first steps in understanding Ubuntu is to get familiar with its installation process. Ubuntu offers a straightforward installation experience, whether you are setting it up on a physical machine or a virtual environment. The installation media, typically a bootable USB or DVD, provides a graphical installer that guides you through language selection, keyboard layout, and partitioning options. You can choose to install Ubuntu alongside another operating system, replace an existing OS, or configure custom partitions. During installation, you'll also set up a user account and configure basic system settings.

Once installed, you'll be greeted by the GNOME desktop environment, the default for Ubuntu. GNOME is designed for simplicity and ease of use, featuring a clean interface with a top bar, a side dock, and an activities overview. The top bar provides access to system settings, notifications, and the clock. The side dock hosts frequently used applications and open windows, while the activities overview offers an overview of all running applications and workspaces. Understanding how to navigate and customize the GNOME desktop will enhance your Ubuntu experience.

Ubuntu's package management system is another critical aspect to understand. Ubuntu uses APT (Advanced Package Tool) for managing software packages. APT handles the installation, upgrade, and removal of software, ensuring that dependencies are resolved automatically. The primary command-line tool for APT is **apt**, which is used for various package management tasks. For instance, **sudo apt update** refreshes the package list, ensuring that you have the latest information about available software. Following this, **sudo apt upgrade** upgrades all installed packages to their latest versions. To install new software, **sudo apt install package_name** retrieves and installs the specified package along with any necessary dependencies.

Ubuntu repositories are collections of software packages available for installation. The main repository includes free and open-source software supported by Canonical, while the universe repository contains community-maintained software. Restricted and multiverse repositories offer proprietary software and non-free applications. Understanding these repositories and how to enable or disable them using the **software-properties-gtk** tool or editing the **/etc/apt/sources.list** file allows you to control the software sources for your system.

Another vital component of Ubuntu is its update and upgrade process. Regular updates keep your system secure and stable. The **apt** command facilitates these updates, and for more significant upgrades, such as moving from one LTS version to another, Ubuntu provides the **do-release-upgrade** tool. This tool automates the upgrade process, ensuring that your system transitions smoothly between major releases. It's essential to understand how to use these tools to maintain an up-to-date system.

Ubuntu also offers extensive hardware support, including drivers for various devices. The **Additional Drivers** tool, accessible from the system settings, helps you manage proprietary drivers for your hardware, such as graphics cards and Wi-Fi adapters. This tool detects available drivers and allows you to install or switch between them, ensuring optimal performance and compatibility with your hardware.

Networking in Ubuntu is another critical area. The NetworkManager utility provides an intuitive interface for managing network connections, including wired, wireless, and VPN connections. The graphical NetworkManager applet, found in the system tray, allows you to connect to networks, configure network settings, and troubleshoot connectivity issues. For advanced network configurations, the **nmcli** command-line tool provides comprehensive control over NetworkManager's capabilities. Understanding how to configure and manage network connections ensures that your system remains connected and accessible.

Ubuntu's security features are designed to protect your system from threats. The Uncomplicated Firewall (UFW) offers a straightforward interface for configuring firewall rules, enhancing network security. By default, UFW is disabled, but it can be enabled and managed using simple commands. For example, **sudo ufw enable** activates the firewall, while **sudo ufw allow**

22/tcp allows SSH traffic through the firewall. Additionally, Ubuntu supports AppArmor, a security module that confines programs to a limited set of resources. AppArmor profiles define the access permissions for applications, enhancing system security.

The Ubuntu Software Center, a graphical application for managing software, simplifies the installation and removal of software packages. The Software Center provides access to thousands of applications, categorized for easy browsing. It also supports installing Snap packages, a universal packaging format developed by Canonical. Snaps are self-contained applications that include all necessary dependencies, allowing them to run on any Linux distribution that supports Snapd. Understanding how to use the Software Center and Snap packages expands the range of available software for your system.

Another useful tool in Ubuntu is the Timeshift utility, which allows you to create and manage system snapshots. Timeshift provides a way to restore your system to a previous state, which is invaluable for recovering from system failures or configuration errors. Snapshots can be scheduled to run automatically or created manually, and they can be stored on local or external storage. Understanding how to configure and use Timeshift ensures that you have a reliable backup and recovery solution.

Simply put, learning Ubuntu entails becoming acquainted with its installation method, desktop environment, package management system, upgrade and upgrade methods, hardware support, networking capabilities, security features, software management tools, and community resources. Once you've mastered these concepts, you'll be prepared to dive deeper into advanced Linux system management and use Ubuntu successfully for diverse openings.

Navigating the Linux Filesystem

An essential ability for efficient system interaction and management is the ability to navigate the Linux filesystem. Beginning with the root directory, denoted by a forward slash (/), the Linux filesystem is structured hierarchically. A structure similar to a tree is created with all the files and directories emanating from this root. In order to make the most of this filesystem, let us get into the nitty-gritty details and execute some useful commands.

At the top of the hierarchy is the root directory (/), which contains several important subdirectories. Some of the key directories include:

- **/bin**: Contains essential binary executables, like basic commands (**ls**, **cp**, **mv**).
- **/etc**: Stores system configuration files.
- **/home**: Contains personal directories for each user.
- **/var**: Holds variable data like logs and spool files.
- **/usr**: Houses user-installed software and libraries.

- **/tmp**: Temporary files created by system and users.

Understanding these directories helps you locate files and perform administrative tasks.

When navigating the filesystem, certain special characters and notations are useful. The dot (.) represents the current directory, while the double dot (..) represents the parent directory. For example, if you are in **/home/user/documents** and you execute **cd ..**, you will move up to **/home/user**.

To print the current working directory, use the **pwd** (print working directory) command. This command shows your current location in the filesystem. For instance:

```
$ pwd

/home/user/documents
```

Changing directories is done with the **cd** (change directory) command. If you want to move to a different directory, you can specify the path to that directory. For example:

```
$ cd /etc
```

This command moves you to the **/etc** directory. If you want to return to your home directory from anywhere in the filesystem, simply use **cd** without any arguments:

```
$ cd
```

Or use the tilde (~) which is a shortcut for your home directory:

```
$ cd ~
```

Both commands will take you back to **/home/yourusername**.

To list the contents of a directory, the **ls** command is used. This command can display files and subdirectories within the current directory. By default, **ls** will show a basic list. Adding the **-l** option will provide a detailed list, including permissions, number of links, owner, group, size, and modification time:

```
$ ls -l

total 12
```

```
drwxr-xr-x 2 user user 4096 Jan 1 10:00 documents
-rw-r--r-- 1 user user 88 Jan 1 10:00 file.txt
```

To view hidden files, which are files starting with a dot (.), use the **-a** option:

```
$ ls -a
. .. .bashrc documents file.txt
```

The **.** and **..** entries you see represent the current and parent directories respectively.

Creating and managing directories is straightforward with commands like **mkdir** (make directory) and **rmdir** (remove directory). To create a new directory:

```
$ mkdir new_directory
```

To remove an empty directory:

```
$ rmdir new_directory
```

If the directory is not empty, you'll need to use **rm** with the **-r** (recursive) option to remove it and all its contents:

```
$ rm -r new_directory
```

Navigating between directories and managing files can also be done using relative and absolute paths. A relative path is specified in relation to the current directory, while an absolute path is specified from the root directory. For example, if you are in **/home/user** and you want to navigate to **/home/user/documents**, you can use either the relative path:

```
$ cd documents
```

Or the absolute path:

```
$ cd /home/user/documents
```

Understanding these path concepts is crucial for efficient navigation and file management.

We shall practice some common navigation scenarios. Assume you are in your home directory (**/home/user**) and you want to list the contents of the **/etc** directory, move to **/var/log**, and then return to your home directory. Following are the commands you would use:

```
$ ls /etc

$ cd /var/log

$ pwd

$ cd
```

This sequence lists the contents of **/etc**, changes the directory to **/var/log**, prints the current directory to confirm the location, and then returns to the home directory.

Additionally, the tab completion feature is incredibly useful. When you start typing a command or path, pressing the Tab key will auto-complete the command or show possible completions if there is more than one match.

For example:

```
$ cd /etc/sys<Tab>
```

Pressing Tab after **sys** will auto-complete to **/etc/systemd/** if it is the only match, or show all matches if there are multiple directories starting with **sys**.

Another useful command is **tree**, which visually displays the directory structure. If **tree** is not installed, you can install it using:

```
$ sudo apt install tree
```

Then, to view the directory structure from the current directory:

```
$ tree
```

This command provides a hierarchical view of directories and subdirectories, making it easier to understand the filesystem layout.

The **find** command helps you locate files and directories. It's particularly useful when you're not sure where something is located. For example, to find a file named **file.txt** starting from the root directory:

```
$ sudo find / -name file.txt
```

This command searches the entire filesystem for **file.txt**, displaying the path if it exists.

The **locate** command is another powerful search tool, using a database of indexed files. It's faster than **find** but requires updating the database periodically using **updatedb**. To find a file using **locate**:

```
$ locate file.txt
```

If the database is up-to-date, this command will quickly display the paths to **file.txt**.

Understanding symbolic links (symlinks) is also important. A symlink is a file that points to another file or directory. Creating a symlink uses the **ln -s** command. For example, to create a symlink to **/etc/passwd** in your home directory:

```
$ ln -s /etc/passwd mypasswd
```

Here, **mypasswd** in your home directory points to **/etc/passwd**. You can use **ls -l** to verify:

```
$ ls -l mypasswd

lrwxrwxrwx 1 user user 12 Jan 1 12:00 mypasswd ->
/etc/passwd
```

Symlinks are useful for creating shortcuts and simplifying file management.

Additionally, there are tools like **find**, **locate**, and **tree**, along with symbolic links, that enhance your ability to manage and navigate the filesystem efficiently.

Basic Linux Commands

Being well-versed in a core set of commands is critical for Linux system administrators to efficiently manage and troubleshoot systems. Let us take a look at a few of the most common commands that each system administrator should know. Some examples of these are commands for system monitoring, process management tools, and network utilities. We'll go over the basics of each command, what it does, and some examples to help you put it all together.

Network Configuration and Troubleshooting

'ip' and 'ifconfig'

The **ip** command is a powerful tool for network configuration. It can replace the older **ifconfig** command, offering more features and flexibility. The **ip** command allows you to view and configure network interfaces, routing tables, and more. To view network interfaces and their details, use:

```
$ ip addr
```

This command lists all network interfaces with their IP addresses and other details. To bring an interface up or down, use:

```
$ sudo ip link set eth0 up

$ sudo ip link set eth0 down
```

The **ifconfig** command, though older, is still widely used. To display network interfaces, you can use:

```
$ ifconfig
```

To configure an IP address on an interface with **ifconfig**:

```
$ sudo ifconfig eth0 192.168.1.100 netmask 255.255.255.0
```

Both commands are useful, but **ip** is recommended for its broader capabilities and modern features.

'mtr'

The **mtr** (My Traceroute) command combines the functionality of **ping** and **traceroute**, providing real-time network diagnostics. It helps identify where packet loss and latency occur. To use **mtr**, simply enter:

```
$ mtr gitforgits.com
```

This command starts a continuous network diagnostic to the specified domain, showing each hop and its performance metrics.

File and Text Processing

'find'

The **find** command searches for files and directories based on various criteria, such as name, size, or modification date. To search for a file named **file.txt** starting from the root directory, use:

```
$ sudo find / -name file.txt
```

This command searches the entire filesystem and lists all paths to **file.txt**. To find files modified in the last 7 days:

```
$ find /home/user -mtime -7
```

This command searches the **/home/user** directory for files modified within the last week.

'awk'

The **awk** command is a powerful text processing tool, often used for data extraction and reporting. It reads input line by line, splits each line into fields, and processes them based on specified patterns. For example, to print the second field of each line in a file:

```
$ awk '{print $2}' file.txt
```

If you have a CSV file and want to print the first and third columns, you can use:

```
$ awk -F, '{print $1, $3}' file.csv
```

This command uses a comma as the field separator and prints the desired columns.

Network Monitoring and Diagnostics

'tcpdump'

The **tcpdump** command captures network packets and displays them in real-time, useful for network troubleshooting and security analysis. To capture packets on the **eth0** interface, use:

```
$ sudo tcpdump -i eth0
```

To capture and save packets to a file for later analysis:

```
$ sudo tcpdump -i eth0 -w capture.pcap
```

To read the saved capture file, use:

```
$ sudo tcpdump -r capture.pcap
```

'netstat'

The **netstat** command displays network connections, routing tables, interface statistics, and more. To list all active connections and listening ports, use:

```
$ netstat -tuln
```

To display network statistics, such as packets transmitted and received, use:

```
$ netstat -s
```

netstat provides a comprehensive view of your network's current state.

'nslookup'

The **nslookup** command queries DNS to obtain domain name or IP address mapping. It's useful for troubleshooting DNS issues. To find the IP address of a domain:

```
$ nslookup gitforgits.com
```

To perform a reverse lookup, converting an IP address to a domain name:

```
$ nslookup 192.168.1.1
```

This command queries the DNS server for the corresponding domain name.

System and Process Management

'sudo'

The **sudo** command allows users to execute commands with superuser privileges, necessary for performing administrative tasks. To edit a system file with superuser permissions:

```
$ sudo nano /etc/hosts
```

To execute a command as another user, specify the **-u** option:

```
$ sudo -u username command
```

sudo is essential for managing system configurations and installing software.

'tmux'

The **tmux** command is a terminal multiplexer that enables you to run multiple terminal sessions within a single window. It's useful for managing multiple tasks without opening several terminal windows. To start a new session:

```
$ tmux
```

To detach from the session while keeping it running, use **Ctrl+b** followed by **d**. To reattach to the session:

```
$ tmux attach
```

tmux helps you organize and switch between tasks efficiently.

'lsns'

The **lsns** command lists information about system namespaces, which are used for isolation in Linux containers and virtual environments. To display all namespaces:

```
$ lsns
```

This command shows the PID, type, and other details of each namespace, useful for managing and troubleshooting containerized applications.

'pkill'

The **pkill** command sends signals to processes based on their name or other attributes. It's commonly used to terminate processes. To kill all processes named **example**:

```
$ pkill example
```

To send a specific signal, such as **SIGKILL** (kill signal):

```
$ pkill -9 example
```

pkill provides a straightforward way to manage running processes.

Email and Web Requests

'mail'

The **mail** command sends and receives emails from the command line, useful for scripting and automated notifications. To send an email:

```
$ echo "This is the body" | mail -s "Subject"
user@gitforgits.com
```

To read received emails:

```
$ mail
```

This command lists the inbox messages, which you can navigate using commands within the **mail** interface.

'curl'

The **curl** command transfers data to or from a server, supporting various protocols like HTTP, FTP, and more. To download a file from a URL:

```
$ curl -O http://gitforgits.com/file.txt
```

To send a GET request and display the response:

```
$ curl http://gitforgits.com
```

For a POST request with data:

```
$ curl -d "param1=value1&param2=value2" -X POST
http://gitforgits.com
```

curl is a versatile tool for web interactions and API testing.

'watch'

The **watch** command runs a command at regular intervals, displaying the output and highlighting changes. It's useful for monitoring system status or command output over time. To repeatedly execute **df -h** and show disk usage:

```
$ watch df -h
```

To run a custom script every two seconds:

```
$ watch -n 2 ./myscript.sh
```

watch helps you keep an eye on changing data and system performance.

Sample Program: Putting All Commands Together

Now that we know how these commands work in theoretical terms, let us see them in action by implementing a number of instances.

Network Configuration and Diagnostics

After configuring a network interface with **ip** or **ifconfig**, use **mtr** to diagnose network issues:

```
$ sudo ip addr add 192.168.1.100/24 dev eth0

$ sudo ip link set eth0 up

$ mtr google.com
```

In the above code snippet, you set an IP address for **eth0**, bring it up, and start a traceroute to Google.

Searching and Processing Files

Search for all **.log** files modified in the last 7 days and print specific columns using **find** and **awk**:

```
$ find /var/log -name "*.log" -mtime -7 | awk -F/ '{print
$NF}'
```

This command lists log files and prints their names.

Capturing and Analyzing Network Traffic

Capture network traffic on **eth0** and analyze the output:

```
$ sudo tcpdump -i eth0 -w traffic.pcap

$ sudo tcpdump -r traffic.pcap
```

This command captures packets and reads the capture file.

DNS Queries and Network Statistics

Query the DNS for a domain and check network connections:

```
$ nslookup gitforgits.com

$ netstat -tuln
```

This shows DNS information and active network connections.

System and Process Management

Use **sudo** to edit a system file, manage sessions with **tmux**, and kill a process:

```
$ sudo nano /etc/fstab

$ tmux

$ pkill myprocess
```

This sequence edits a configuration file, starts a new tmux session, and terminates a process.

Email and Web Requests

Send an email and download a file using **mail** and **curl**:

```
$ echo "Report is ready" | mail -s "Report Notification"
admin@gitforgits.com

$ curl -O http://gitforgits.com/report.pdf
```

This sends a notification email and downloads a file.

Monitoring System Changes

Use **watch** to monitor disk usage:

```
$ watch df -h
```

This continuously displays disk usage every two seconds.

All sorts of administrative and troubleshooting tasks rely on these commands, which let you operate systems efficiently and effectively. Your command-line skills will greatly improve as you incorporate them into your routine tasks and have increased proficiency in administering Linux settings.

File and Directory Management

Take on the role of a tech company's system administrator. It is your responsibility to establish the directory structure for the new project "AlphaProject." Developers, designers, and quality assurance testers are all part of separate teams that need to work together on this project. Access requirements vary per team. It is your responsibility to oversee the organization of this directory, set permissions, and make sure everything runs smoothly and securely.

Setting up the Directory Structure

First, let us create the main directory and subdirectories for each team within the project. Use the **mkdir** command:

```
$ mkdir -p
/projects/AlphaProject/{developers,designers,qa}
```

This command creates the main directory **/projects/AlphaProject** and three subdirectories: **developers**, **designers**, and **qa**, all in one go.

Creating Files and Directories

Within these directories, you will create some files and further subdirectories. For example, the developers need a subdirectory for scripts:

```
$ mkdir /projects/AlphaProject/developers/scripts
```

And the designers need a directory for assets:

```
$ mkdir /projects/AlphaProject/designers/assets
```

You can also create files using the **touch** command:

```
$ touch /projects/AlphaProject/developers/scripts/init.sh

$ touch /projects/AlphaProject/designers/assets/logo.png
```

These commands create an empty script file and an image file.

Accessing Hidden Files and Directories

Hidden files and directories in Linux start with a dot (**.**). To list all files, including hidden ones, use the **ls -a** command:

```
$ ls -a /projects/AlphaProject/developers

. .. scripts .hidden_config
```

This lists all files, including **.hidden_config**.

Viewing File and Directory Permissions

Permissions in Linux are crucial for controlling access. Use the **ls -l** command to view detailed information, including permissions:

```
$ ls -l /projects/AlphaProject/developers/scripts
```

```
total 0
-rw-r--r-- 1 user group 0 Jan 1 12:00 init.sh
```

The output shows the permissions, owner, and group for each file.

Changing File and Directory Permissions

To modify permissions, use the **chmod** command. For instance, to give execute permission to the script file:

```
$ chmod +x
/projects/AlphaProject/developers/scripts/init.sh
```

You can also set specific permissions using numeric mode. For example, setting read, write, and execute permissions for the owner, and read and execute for the group and others:

```
$ chmod 755
/projects/AlphaProject/developers/scripts/init.sh
```

This command sets the permissions as **rwxr-xr-x**.

Setting Ownership

Use the **chown** command to change the owner and group of a file or directory. For instance, to set the owner to **devuser** and the group to **devgroup**:

```
$ sudo chown devuser:devgroup
/projects/AlphaProject/developers/scripts/init.sh
```

This command changes the owner and group accordingly.

Accessing Secured Files

Sometimes, you need to access files with restricted permissions. Use **sudo** to execute commands with superuser privileges:

```
$ sudo cat /etc/securefile
```

This command allows you to view the contents of a file that requires elevated permissions.

Understanding Permissions and Access Control

To understand who has access to a file or directory, look at the permissions output. The permissions string (e.g., **-rwxr-xr-x**) consists of:

- A type indicator (**-** for files, **d** for directories)
- Owner permissions (rwx)
- Group permissions (r-x)
- Others permissions (r-x)

Each set of permissions is represented by three characters: read (**r**), write (**w**), and execute (**x**). A dash (**-**) means the permission is not granted.

For example, if you see:

```
$ ls -l /projects/AlphaProject/developers/scripts/init.sh

-rwxr-xr-x 1 devuser devgroup 0 Jan 1 12:00 init.sh
```

It means the owner **devuser** has read, write, and execute permissions, the group **devgroup** has read and execute permissions, and others also have read and execute permissions.

Managing Large Files and Directories

Sometimes, you need to handle large files or directories. Use the **du** (disk usage) command to check the size of directories:

```
$ du -sh /projects/AlphaProject/
```

This command gives a summary of the disk usage in a human-readable format.

To find the largest files and directories, use:

```
$ du -ah /projects/AlphaProject/ | sort -rh | head -n 10
```

This command lists the top 10 largest files and directories within **AlphaProject**.

Moving and Copying Files

Use the **mv** command to move or rename files and directories. For instance, to move a script to a different directory:

```
$ mv /projects/AlphaProject/developers/scripts/init.sh
/projects/AlphaProject/qa/
```

To rename a directory:

```
$ mv /projects/AlphaProject/developers/scripts
/projects/AlphaProject/developers/tools
```

The **cp** command copies files and directories. To copy a file:

```
$ cp /projects/AlphaProject/designers/assets/logo.png
/projects/AlphaProject/qa/
```

To copy an entire directory, use the **-r** (recursive) option:

```
$ cp -r /projects/AlphaProject/developers
/projects/Backup/
```

This command copies the **developers** directory and its contents to **/projects/Backup**.

Deleting Files and Directories

To remove files, use the **rm** command. For example, to delete a file:

```
$ rm /projects/AlphaProject/qa/init.sh
```

To remove an empty directory, use **rmdir**:

```
$ rmdir /projects/AlphaProject/qa/temp
```

To remove a directory and its contents, use **rm -r**:

```
$ rm -r /projects/AlphaProject/qa/temp
```

Finding Files Based on Permissions

Sometimes, you might need to find files with specific permissions. Use the **find** command for this purpose. For example, to find all files with 777 permissions:

```
$ find /projects/AlphaProject -type f -perm 0777
```

This command searches for files with read, write, and execute permissions for everyone.

Working with Links

Linux supports symbolic (soft) and hard links. A symbolic link is like a shortcut to another file, while a hard link is an additional name for an existing file. To create a symbolic link:

```
$ ln -s /projects/AlphaProject/designers/assets/logo.png
/projects/AlphaProject/logo_link.png
```

To create a hard link:

```
$ ln /projects/AlphaProject/developers/scripts/init.sh
/projects/AlphaProject/init_link.sh
```

Symbolic links can point to directories, while hard links cannot. Use **ls -l** to view link details:

```
$ ls -l /projects/AlphaProject/logo_link.png

lrwxrwxrwx 1 user group 40 Jan 1 12:00
/projects/AlphaProject/logo_link.png ->
/projects/AlphaProject/designers/assets/logo.png
```

Archiving and Compressing Files

To archive and compress files, use the **tar** command. Create a tarball (compressed archive) of the project directory:

```
$ tar -czvf /projects/AlphaProject.tar.gz
/projects/AlphaProject
```

To extract the contents of a tarball:

```
$ tar -xzvf /projects/AlphaProject.tar.gz -C /projects/
```

The **-c** option creates an archive, **-x** extracts it, **-z** compresses/uncompresses with gzip, **-v** shows progress, and **-f** specifies the filename.

File Integrity and Security

To ensure file integrity, use the **md5sum** or **sha256sum** commands. Generate a checksum for a file:

```
$ md5sum /projects/AlphaProject/designers/assets/logo.png

d41d8cd98f00b204e9800998ecf8427e
/projects/AlphaProject/designers/assets/logo.png
```

This command outputs a unique hash, which can be used to verify the file's integrity later.

Scheduling Regular Tasks

To automate file and directory management tasks, use **crontab** to schedule commands. Edit the crontab file:

```
$ crontab -e
```

Add a job to back up the project directory every day at midnight:

```
0 0 * * * tar -czvf /backup/AlphaProject_$(date
+\%F).tar.gz /projects/AlphaProject
```

This cron job creates a compressed backup with the current date in the filename.

Monitoring File and Directory Changes

To monitor changes in real-time, use **inotifywait** from the **inotify-tools** package. Install it using:

```
$ sudo apt install inotify-tools
```

Monitor changes in the project directory:

```
$ inotifywait -m /projects/AlphaProject
```

This command watches for modifications, deletions, and other events in the specified directory.

Through the real-world example of organizing a project's directory structure, you discovered how to safely handle files, see and change permissions, create and manage directories, and access hidden files. These abilities, which will be expanded upon in later chapters, are fundamental for efficient system administration. As you go along, keep in mind that the "AlphaProject" is a great way to put everything you've learned into practice and deepen your comprehension of these commands.

Introduction to Shell

The shell is a crucial component of the Linux operating system, serving as the interface between the user and the kernel. It allows users to execute commands, run scripts, and automate tasks. The shell interprets user input and translates it into actions performed by the system. There are various types of shells available in Linux, such as Bash (Bourne Again Shell), Zsh, and Fish, but Bash is the most widely used and is considered the best shell for system administrators due to its robust features and extensive scripting capabilities.

Purpose of Shell

The primary purpose of the shell is to provide an environment where users can interact with the operating system. It facilitates the execution of commands, running of programs, and manipulation of files and directories. The shell also supports scripting, enabling users to automate repetitive tasks, schedule jobs, and create complex workflows. When a user types a command in the terminal, the shell interprets it and communicates with the kernel to perform the requested action.

Introducing Bash

Bash, short for Bourne Again Shell, is an enhanced version of the original Unix shell (sh). It is the default shell on most Linux distributions, including Ubuntu. Bash provides powerful features like command history, tab completion, and scripting capabilities, making it an excellent choice for system administrators.

To start using Bash, you simply open a terminal window. In most Linux distributions, Bash is the default shell, so you don't need to do anything special to start it. You can check the current shell with the following command:

```
$ echo $SHELL

/bin/bash
```

This command outputs the path to the current shell, confirming that you are using Bash.

Basic Bash Commands

We shall start with some basic commands to get familiar with Bash. These commands will help you navigate the filesystem, manage files, and execute programs.

Navigating Directories

Use the **cd** command to change directories:

```
$ cd /projects/AlphaProject

$ pwd

/projects/AlphaProject
```

Listing Directory Contents

The **ls** command lists the contents of a directory:

```
$ ls

developers designers qa
```

Add **-l** for a detailed listing:

```
$ ls -l

total 12

drwxr-xr-x 2 user user 4096 Jan 1 12:00 developers

drwxr-xr-x 2 user user 4096 Jan 1 12:00 designers

drwxr-xr-x 2 user user 4096 Jan 1 12:00 qa
```

Creating and Deleting Files

Use the **touch** command to create an empty file and **rm** to delete it:

```
$ touch testfile.txt

$ ls

developers designers qa testfile.txt

$ rm testfile.txt
```

Copying and Moving Files

The **cp** command copies files, and **mv** moves or renames them:

```
$ cp /projects/AlphaProject/designers/assets/logo.png
/projects/AlphaProject/qa/

$ mv /projects/AlphaProject/qa/logo.png
/projects/AlphaProject/qa/logo_backup.png
```

Using Command History

One of the convenient features of Bash is command history. Bash keeps a record of previously executed commands, which you can access using the up and down arrow keys. This feature saves time and reduces errors by allowing you to quickly repeat or modify previous commands.

To view the command history, use:

```
$ history
```

This command lists all previously executed commands with their respective numbers. You can rerun a command by typing **!** followed by the command number:

```
$ !10
```

This reruns the command listed as number 10 in the history.

Tab Completion

Bash supports tab completion, which speeds up typing and reduces errors. When you start typing a command, file name, or directory name, pressing the Tab key will auto-complete the text or show possible completions. For example:

```
$ cd /projects/AlphaProject/developers/sc<Tab>
```

If there is only one directory that starts with **sc**, Bash will auto-complete it to **scripts**. If there are multiple matches, pressing Tab again will display all possibilities.

Bash Variables

Bash allows you to create and use variables to store data. Variables can hold text, numbers, or command output. To create a variable, simply assign a value to it:

```
$ PROJECT_DIR=/projects/AlphaProject
```

To use the variable, prefix it with a dollar sign (**$**):

```
$ cd $PROJECT_DIR

$ pwd

/projects/AlphaProject
```

Variables are useful for storing paths, filenames, and other data that you frequently use in your scripts or commands.

Bash Scripting

Bash scripting enables you to automate tasks by writing scripts that execute a series of commands. A Bash script is simply a text file with a **.sh** extension that contains Bash commands.

To create a basic script,

- Open a text editor and enter the following lines:

```
#!/bin/bash

echo "Hello, AlphaProject!"
```

- Save the file as **hello.sh**.

- Make the script executable:

```
$ chmod +x hello.sh
```

- Run the script:

```
$ ./hello.sh

Hello, AlphaProject!
```

The **#!/bin/bash** line at the top is called a shebang and indicates that the script should be run using Bash. The **echo** command prints the text to the terminal.

Conditional Statements

Bash scripts can include conditional statements to perform different actions based on conditions. The **if** statement is used to test conditions:

```
#!/bin/bash

if [ -d "/projects/AlphaProject" ]; then

 echo "AlphaProject directory exists."

else

 echo "AlphaProject directory does not exist."

fi
```

Save this script as **check_dir.sh**, make it executable, and run it:

```
$ chmod +x check_dir.sh

$ ./check_dir.sh

AlphaProject directory exists.
```

The **-d** option checks if the specified path is a directory.

Loops in Bash

Loops allow you to execute a set of commands multiple times. The **for** loop iterates over a list of items:

```
#!/bin/bash

for team in developers designers qa; do

 echo "Setting up $team directory..."

 mkdir -p /projects/AlphaProject/$team

done
```

Save this script as **setup_teams.sh**, make it executable, and run it:

```
$ chmod +x setup_teams.sh

$ ./setup_teams.sh

Setting up developers directory...

Setting up designers directory...

Setting up qa directory...
```

This script creates directories for each team in the AlphaProject.

The **while** loop runs as long as a condition is true:

```
#!/bin/bash

count=1

while [ $count -le 5 ]; do

 echo "Count: $count"

 ((count++))
```

```
done
```

Save this script as **count.sh**, make it executable, and run it:

```
$ chmod +x count.sh

$ ./count.sh

Count: 1

Count: 2

Count: 3

Count: 4

Count: 5
```

This script counts from 1 to 5, demonstrating the use of a **while** loop.

Functions in Bash

Functions in Bash allow you to group commands and reuse them. Define a function by using the **function** keyword followed by the function name and curly braces:

```
#!/bin/bash

function greet {

 echo "Hello, $1!"

}

greet AlphaProject
```

Save this script as **greet.sh**, make it executable, and run it:

```
$ chmod +x greet.sh
```

```
$ ./greet.sh
Hello, AlphaProject!
```

This script defines a **greet** function that takes an argument and prints a greeting message.

All system administrators must possess these skills, as they will provide the basis for the more advanced topics covered in the sections that follow. As we move on with the AlphaProject use-case, you'll discover the practical applications of Bash's capabilities, which will boost your skills and self-assurance when it comes to administering Linux systems.

Basics of Package Management

Purpose of Managing Packages

A package manager automates the process of managing software packages, including resolving dependencies, downloading, and configuring software. The AlphaProject team is utilizing Ubuntu, which comes with its default package manager being the Advanced Package Tool (APT). Package management's principal objective is to streamline program installation, upgrade, and removal processes. It checks that the software integrates correctly with the system and that all dependencies are met. Additionally, package management makes it easier to apply updates and patches, which helps to maintain the system secure and reliable.

Updating Package Lists and Upgrading Software

Before installing or upgrading packages, it is essential to update the package list, which ensures that you have the latest information about available software. Use the following command to update the package list:

```
$ sudo apt update
```

This command fetches the latest package information from the repositories configured on your system.

After updating the package list, you can upgrade all installed packages to their latest versions with:

```
$ sudo apt upgrade
```

This command downloads and installs updates for all installed packages. If you want to upgrade only specific packages, you can specify them:

```
$ sudo apt upgrade package_name
```

For a more comprehensive upgrade that also removes obsolete packages, use:

```
$ sudo apt full-upgrade
```

Installing Packages

To install a new package, use the **apt install** command. For instance, if you need to install Git for the AlphaProject, you would run:

```
$ sudo apt install git
```

APT resolves and installs any dependencies required by Git, ensuring that it works correctly on your system.

Viewing Installed Packages

To view a list of all installed packages, use the **dpkg --list** command:

```
$ dpkg --list
```

This command displays a detailed list of installed packages, including their names, versions, and descriptions.

If you need to find information about a specific package, use **apt show** followed by the package name. For example, to view details about Git:

```
$ apt show git
```

This command provides detailed information about the Git package, including its dependencies, description, and installed version.

Deleting Packages

To remove a package that is no longer needed, use the **apt remove** command:

```
$ sudo apt remove package_name
```

For example, to remove Git:

```
$ sudo apt remove git
```

If you want to remove a package along with its configuration files, use:

```
$ sudo apt purge package_name
```

For example, to completely remove Git and its configuration files:

```
$ sudo apt purge git
```

After removing packages, it is a good idea to clean up unnecessary dependencies with:

```
$ sudo apt autoremove
```

This command removes packages that were installed as dependencies but are no longer required.

Finding Packages

To search for packages, use the **apt search** command followed by a keyword. For example, to find packages related to Python, you would run:

```
$ apt search python
```

This command lists all packages that match the keyword, helping you discover new software that may be useful for your projects.

Working with Repositories

Repositories are locations where packages are stored and from which they can be downloaded and installed. Ubuntu's package manager uses several default repositories, but you can also add custom repositories to access additional software.

To add a new repository, use the **add-apt-repository** command. For example, to add a PPA (Personal Package Archive) for the latest version of Node.js:

```
$ sudo add-apt-repository ppa:chris-lea/node.js
```

```
$ sudo apt update

$ sudo apt install nodejs
```

After adding the repository, update the package list to include the new software and then install the desired package.

Pinning Packages

Sometimes, you may want to prevent a package from being updated. This is known as pinning. To pin a package, you create a preferences file in **/etc/apt/preferences.d/**. For example, to pin Git to its current version, create a file named **git** in **/etc/apt/preferences.d/** with the following content:

```
Package: git

Pin: version x.y.z

Pin-Priority: 1001
```

Replace **x.y.z** with the desired version number. This configuration prevents Git from being updated during an upgrade.

Sample Program: Managing Packages for AlphaProject

For the AlphaProject, suppose we need several software tools, such as Git, Node.js, and Docker. Following is how you would manage these packages using APT:

- Update Package List:

```
$ sudo apt update
```

- Install Git:

```
$ sudo apt install git
```

- Install Node.js from a PPA:

```
$ sudo add-apt-repository ppa:chris-lea/node.js
```

```
$ sudo apt update

$ sudo apt install nodejs
```

- Install Docker:
  - First, add Docker's official GPG key and repository:

```
$ sudo apt install apt-transport-https ca-certificates
curl software-properties-common

$ curl -fsSL https://download.docker.com/linux/ubuntu/gpg
| sudo apt-key add -

$ sudo add-apt-repository "deb [arch=amd64]
https://download.docker.com/linux/ubuntu $(lsb_release -
cs) stable"

$ sudo apt update

$ sudo apt install docker-ce
```

- Verify Installations:
  - Check that Git, Node.js, and Docker are installed correctly:

```
$ git --version

git version 2.x.y

$ node --version

v14.x.y

$ docker --version

Docker version 19.x.y, build abcdef
```

- Pin Docker to Prevent Automatic Updates:
  - Create a preferences file for Docker:

```
$ echo -e "Package: docker-ce\nPin: version 19.x.y\nPin-Priority: 1001" | sudo tee /etc/apt/preferences.d/docker-ce
```

- Update All Installed Packages:

```
$ sudo apt upgrade
```

- Remove an Unneeded Package:
  - If you decide to remove Node.js:

```
$ sudo apt remove nodejs

$ sudo apt autoremove
```

All required software tools must be installed, updated, and managed correctly for the AlphaProject. Follow these above procedures to accomplish this.

System Startup and Shutdown

When it comes to managing the stability and performance of your servers, it is necessary to manage the processes involved in starting up and shutting down the system. Specifically for the AlphaProject, we will go over the necessary commands for powering down and starting up systems, as well as how to automate these tasks.

Shutting Down and Rebooting the System

To shut down the system immediately, use the **shutdown** command with the **-h** (halt) option:

```
$ sudo shutdown -h now
```

This command powers off the system immediately. You can also schedule a shutdown at a specific time. For example, to shut down the system at 10:30 PM:

```
$ sudo shutdown -h 22:30
```

If you need to cancel a scheduled shutdown, use:

```
$ sudo shutdown -c
```

To reboot the system, use the **-r** (reboot) option:

```
$ sudo shutdown -r now
```

Alternatively, you can use the **reboot** command directly:

```
$ sudo reboot
```

Booting the System

Booting the system typically involves turning on the machine and allowing it to go through the boot process, which includes loading the bootloader (GRUB), the kernel, and initializing system services. On a remote server, you would usually rely on remote management tools to initiate a reboot if necessary.

Automating Startup and Shutdown

Automation can help ensure that your systems start up and shut down according to a schedule. This is particularly useful for development environments or non-critical systems.

To automate shutdowns, you can use **cron**, a time-based job scheduler in Unix-like operating systems. To schedule a shutdown at midnight every day, edit the crontab file:

```
$ sudo crontab -e
```

Add the following line:

```
0 0 * * * /sbin/shutdown -h now
```

This cron job schedules a system shutdown at midnight daily.

Automating system startups is more complex and depends on your hardware. Some systems support scheduling startups in the BIOS/UEFI settings. Alternatively, you can use Wake-on-LAN (WoL) if your network and hardware support it. To configure WoL, ensure your network interface is set up to receive the wake-up signal. First, install the **ethtool** package:

```
$ sudo apt install ethtool
```

Then enable WoL on your network interface (e.g., **eth0**):

```
$ sudo ethtool -s eth0 wol g
```

To wake up the system, you'll need another machine to send the wake-up signal using a tool like **wakeonlan**:

```
$ sudo apt install wakeonlan
$ wakeonlan <MAC_ADDRESS_OF_TARGET_MACHINE>
```

Replace **<MAC_ADDRESS_OF_TARGET_MACHINE>** with the actual MAC address of the system you want to wake up.

Managing Specific Services

Services are essential parts of your system that perform various functions, such as running web servers, databases, or other background processes. Managing these services effectively ensures that your system runs smoothly.

Starting and Stopping Services

Use the **systemctl** command to manage services. To start a service, use:

```
$ sudo systemctl start service_name
```

For example, to start the Apache web server:

```
$ sudo systemctl start apache2
```

To stop a service, use:

```
$ sudo systemctl stop service_name
```

For example, to stop Apache:

```
$ sudo systemctl stop apache2
```

To restart a service, use:

```
$ sudo systemctl restart service_name
```

To reload the configuration without stopping the service:

```
$ sudo systemctl reload service_name
```

Enabling and Disabling Services at Boot

To ensure a service starts automatically at boot, use the **enable** command:

```
$ sudo systemctl enable service_name
```

To disable a service from starting at boot:

```
$ sudo systemctl disable service_name
```

Checking Service Status

To check the status of a service, use:

```
$ sudo systemctl status service_name
```

This command provides detailed information about the service, including whether it is running, its last startup time, and any recent log entries.

Sample Program: Managing AlphaProject Services

Let us assume AlphaProject requires a web server (Apache) and a database server (MySQL). Following is how you manage these services:

- Start Apache and MySQL:

```
$ sudo systemctl start apache2

$ sudo systemctl start mysql
```

- Ensure Apache and MySQL Start at Boot:

```
$ sudo systemctl enable apache2
```

```
$ sudo systemctl enable mysql
```

- Check the Status of Apache and MySQL:

```
$ sudo systemctl status apache2
$ sudo systemctl status mysql
```

- Stop Apache and MySQL:

```
$ sudo systemctl stop apache2
$ sudo systemctl stop mysql
```

- Restart Apache and MySQL:

```
$ sudo systemctl restart apache2
$ sudo systemctl restart mysql
```

Scheduling Service Management with Cron

In addition to automating shutdowns, you can use **cron** to schedule service management tasks. For instance, if you want to restart Apache every Sunday at 2 AM to ensure it runs smoothly, add a cron job:

```
$ sudo crontab -e
```

Add the following line:

```
0 2 * * 0 /bin/systemctl restart apache2
```

This job restarts Apache every Sunday at 2 AM.

Logging and Monitoring Services

It's important to monitor services and check their logs to troubleshoot issues. Logs are typically stored in the **/var/log** directory. For Apache, logs can be found in:

```
$ ls /var/log/apache2/
```

To view the most recent entries in the Apache error log:

```
$ tail -f /var/log/apache2/error.log
```

The **tail -f** command continuously displays new log entries, making it easier to monitor live activities.

If you want to keep AlphaProject running smoothly, you need to know how the system starts and stops and how to manage individual services. Your system's seamless operation, efficient management of services, and ability to resolve difficulties by monitoring logs are all guaranteed by these skills.

Managing Processes

A process is an instance of a program in execution, and each process has a unique process ID (PID). There are four possible states for a process: running, sleeping, stopped, and zombie. To make sure your system works well and meets user demands, you need to know these states and how to handle processes.

Stages of a Process

1. Running: The process is actively using the CPU.
2. Sleeping: The process is waiting for a resource or event (e.g., I/O operations). This can be further divided into:
    - Interruptible Sleep: The process can be interrupted by signals.
    - Uninterruptible Sleep: The process is waiting for a hardware condition and cannot be interrupted.
3. Stopped: The process has been stopped, usually by a signal or because it is being debugged.
4. Zombie: The process has completed execution, but its parent has not yet read its exit status.

Displaying Running Processes

To view running processes, use the **ps** command, which provides a snapshot of current processes. The **ps aux** command gives a detailed list of all processes:

```
$ ps aux
```

This output includes information such as the user running the process, PID, CPU and memory usage, start time, and command.

For a real-time view of running processes, use the **top** command:

```
$ top
```

top displays an interactive, dynamic view of system processes, which updates every few seconds. It shows CPU and memory usage, process IDs, and other key metrics.

Another powerful tool is **htop**, which is a more user-friendly version of **top**:

```
$ sudo apt install htop

$ htop
```

htop provides a colorful, interactive interface, making it easier to navigate and manage processes.

Starting and Terminating Processes

To start a process, simply run a command. For example, to start the **nano** text editor:

```
$ nano
```

To start a process in the background, append an ampersand (**&**) to the command:

```
$ nano &
```

This runs **nano** in the background, allowing you to continue using the terminal.

To terminate a process, use the **kill** command followed by the PID. First, find the PID using **ps** or **pgrep**:

```
$ pgrep nano

1234
```

```
$ kill 1234
```

If a process does not terminate with a normal **kill** signal, use **kill -9** to forcefully terminate it:

```
$ kill -9 1234
```

Adjusting Process Priority

The **nice** and **renice** commands adjust process priority. Priority ranges from -20 (highest priority) to 19 (lowest priority). To start a process with a specific priority, use **nice**:

```
$ nice -n 10 nano
```

This starts **nano** with a lower priority. To change the priority of an existing process, use **renice** followed by the new priority and PID:

```
$ renice -n 5 -p 1234
```

This command sets the priority of the process with PID 1234 to 5.

Suspending and Resuming Processes

To suspend a process running in the foreground, press **Ctrl+Z**. This stops the process and places it in the background. You can view suspended jobs using the **jobs** command:

```
$ jobs

[1]+ Stopped nano
```

To resume a suspended job in the foreground, use the **fg** command followed by the job number:

```
$ fg %1
```

To resume the job in the background, use **bg**:

```
$ bg %1
```

Monitoring Process Activity

For detailed monitoring of process activity, use **strace**. This tool traces system calls and signals. To monitor a running process:

```
$ sudo strace -p 1234
```

To trace a new process from start:

```
$ strace nano
```

Sample Program: Managing Processes for AlphaProject

We shall consider some practical scenarios for managing processes in the context of AlphaProject:

Starting a Web Server

To start the Apache web server:

```
$ sudo systemctl start apache2
```

Verify it is running:

```
$ sudo systemctl status apache2
```

Running a Background Script

Suppose you have a maintenance script **maintenance.sh** that you want to run in the background:

```
$ ./maintenance.sh &
```

Check the background job:

```
$ jobs

[1]+ Running ./maintenance.sh &
```

Monitoring Web Server Activity

Use **htop** to monitor the Apache server and other processes:

```
$ htop
```

Look for the **apache2** processes to check their resource usage.

Terminating a Misbehaving Process

If a script is consuming too many resources, find its PID and terminate it. For instance, if **maintenance.sh** has PID 5678:

```
$ kill 5678
```

If it doesn't respond:

```
$ kill -9 5678
```

Changing the Priority of a Backup Process

Suppose you are running a backup script **backup.sh** and want to lower its priority to ensure it doesn't affect other services:

```
$ nice -n 10 ./backup.sh &
```

To change the priority of an already running backup process with PID 91011:

```
$ renice -n 15 -p 91011
```

Suspending and Resuming Long-Running Compilation

If you start a compilation process that you need to pause:

```
$ make
```

Press **Ctrl+Z** to suspend it:

```
$ jobs

[1]+ Stopped make
```

Resume it in the background:

```
$ bg %1
```

Automating Process Management with Cron

Schedule a nightly database backup using a cron job. Edit the crontab file:

```
$ sudo crontab -e
```

Add the following line to schedule the backup script to run at 2 AM daily:

```
0 2 * * * /usr/local/bin/backup.sh
```

Monitoring Processes with 'ps' and 'top'

Regularly check the processes using **ps**:

```
$ ps aux | grep apache2
```

Or use **top** for a real-time view:

```
$ top
```

Tracing a Problematic Process

If the web server is misbehaving, trace its system calls:

```
$ sudo strace -p $(pgrep apache2)
```

Using 'lsof' to Check Open Files

If a process is holding onto a file or port, use **lsof** to list open files:

```
$ sudo lsof -i :80
```

This command shows processes listening on port 80.

Sample Workflow: Handling High CPU Usage

Let us say during peak hours, you notice high CPU usage affecting the performance of AlphaProject's web server. Given below is how you can manage this:

Identify the High CPU Process

Use **`top`** or **`htop`** to identify processes consuming high CPU:

```
$ top
```

Look for processes with high **`%CPU`** values.

Adjust the Priority

Suppose the high CPU process has PID 2345. Lower its priority to reduce its CPU consumption:

```
$ sudo renice 10 -p 2345
```

Monitor the Process

Keep an eye on the process to see if the situation improves:

```
$ htop
```

Terminate If Necessary

If lowering the priority doesn't help and the process is non-critical, terminate it:

```
$ sudo kill 2345
```

If it doesn't terminate:

```
$ sudo kill -9 2345
```

These above tools primarily **`ps`**, **`top`**, **`htop`**, **`kill`**, **`nice`**, **`renice`**, and **`strace`** ensure that your services run smoothly, resource usage is optimized, and any misbehaving processes are quickly handled. When we go further into Linux system administration, this background knowledge will help with higher-level tasks and circumstances.

Accessing and using Linux Utilities

Among the many useful tools available to system administrators, Linux utilities are among the most powerful. From text processing and file manipulation to network diagnostics and system monitoring, these utilities do it all.

Role of Utilities

Utilities simplify complex tasks, automate repetitive processes, and provide critical information about the system. They help in managing files, monitoring performance, diagnosing issues, and configuring network settings. By mastering these utilities, you can enhance productivity and ensure the smooth operation of your projects.

Common Utilities for AlphaProject

For AlphaProject, several utilities are particularly useful. These include:

1. File and Directory Management: **cp**, **mv**, **rm**, **find**
2. Text Processing: **grep**, **sed**, **awk**
3. Network Utilities: **ping**, **traceroute**, **netstat**, **curl**
4. System Monitoring: **top**, **htop**, **df**, **du**
5. Archiving and Compression: **tar**, **gzip**, **zip**
6. Disk Usage and Partition Management: **df**, **du**, **fdisk**, **lsblk**

We shall explore these utilities and learn how to use them practically for managing AlphaProject.

File and Directory Management Utilities

'cp', 'mv', and 'rm'

These commands are fundamental for managing files and directories.

To copy files:

```
$ cp /projects/AlphaProject/developers/scripts/init.sh
/projects/AlphaProject/backup/
```

To move files:

```
$ mv /projects/AlphaProject/backup/init.sh
/projects/AlphaProject/qa/
```

To remove files:

```
$ rm /projects/AlphaProject/qa/init.sh
```

'find'

The **find** command is invaluable for locating files based on various criteria. For example, to find all **.sh** files in the AlphaProject directory:

```
$ find /projects/AlphaProject -name "*.sh"
```

Text Processing Utilities

'grep'

The **grep** command searches for patterns within files. To search for the word "error" in log files:

```
$ grep "error" /projects/AlphaProject/logs/*.log
```

'sed'

The **sed** (stream editor) command performs basic text transformations on an input stream. To replace "foo" with "bar" in a file:

```
$ sed -i 's/foo/bar/g'
/projects/AlphaProject/developers/config.txt
```

'awk'

The **awk** command is used for pattern scanning and processing. To print the second column of a CSV file:

```
$ awk -F, '{print $2}' /projects/AlphaProject/data.csv
```

Network Utilities

'ping'

The **ping** command checks network connectivity to a host. To ping google.com:

```
$ ping google.com
```

'traceroute'

The **traceroute** command traces the path packets take to reach a network host. To trace the route to google.com:

```
$ traceroute google.com
```

'netstat'

The **netstat** command displays network connections, routing tables, interface statistics, and more. To list all active network connections:

```
$ netstat -tuln
```

'curl'

The **curl** command transfers data from or to a server using various protocols. To download a file from a URL:

```
$ curl -O http://gitforgits.com/file.txt
```

System Monitoring Utilities

'top' and 'htop'

These commands display real-time system statistics.

To use **top**:

```
$ top
```

For a more user-friendly interface, use **htop**:

```
$ htop
```

'df' and 'du'

These commands display disk space usage.

To check disk space usage:

```
$ df -h
```

To check directory size:

```
$ du -sh /projects/AlphaProject
```

Archiving and Compression Utilities

'tar', 'gzip', and 'zip'

These commands manage file archives and compression.

To create a tarball:

```
$ tar -czvf /projects/AlphaProject.tar.gz
/projects/AlphaProject
```

To extract a tarball:

```
$ tar -xzvf /projects/AlphaProject.tar.gz -C /projects/
```

To compress a file with **gzip**:

```
$ gzip /projects/AlphaProject/data.txt
```

To decompress:

```
$ gunzip /projects/AlphaProject/data.txt.gz
```

To zip a directory:

```
$ zip -r /projects/AlphaProject.zip
/projects/AlphaProject
```

Disk Usage and Partition Management Utilities

'fdisk' and 'lsblk'

These commands manage disk partitions and list block devices.

To list partitions:

```
$ sudo fdisk -l
```

To display block devices:

```
$ lsblk
```

Sample Program: Using Utilities in AlphaProject

We shall apply these utilities to our AlphaProject use-case:

File Backup and Management

Create a backup of the **developers** directory:

```
$ cp -r /projects/AlphaProject/developers
/projects/AlphaProject/backup/
```

Log Analysis

Search for errors in log files:

```
$ grep "error" /projects/AlphaProject/logs/*.log
```

Configuration Management

Update configuration settings in **config.txt**:

```
$ sed -i 's/old_value/new_value/g'
/projects/AlphaProject/developers/config.txt
```

Network Diagnostics

Check network connectivity to a remote server:

```
$ ping server.gitforgits.com
```

System Monitoring

Monitor system performance using **htop**:

```
$ htop
```

Disk Space Management

Check available disk space:

```
$ df -h
```

Archiving Project Data

Create a compressed archive of the project:

```
$ tar -czvf /projects/AlphaProject_backup.tar.gz
/projects/AlphaProject
```

Downloading Resources

Download a script from a remote server:

```
$ curl -O http://gitforgits.com/script.sh
```

Disk Partition Analysis

List disk partitions:

```
$ sudo fdisk -l
```

All these above utilities—**cp**, **mv**, **rm**, **find**, **grep**, **sed**, **awk**, **ping**, **traceroute**, **netstat**, **curl**, **top**, **htop**, **df**, **du**, **tar**, **gzip**, **zip**, **fdisk**, and **lsblk** allows to manage files, process text, diagnose network issues, monitor systems, and manage disk space.

Summary

In this chapter, we explored foundational concepts and practical skills essential for Linux system administration, focusing on our AlphaProject use-case. We started by understanding Linux Ubuntu, its installation process, and the GNOME desktop environment, which provided a user-friendly interface for navigating the system. Navigating the Linux filesystem was covered extensively, teaching how to use commands like **cd**, **ls**, and **pwd** to move through directories and manage files. We also delved into viewing and modifying file permissions using **chmod** and **chown**, understanding symbolic links with **ln**, and handling hidden files with **ls -a**.

Basic Linux commands were introduced, including **ip** and **ifconfig** for network configuration, **mtr** for network diagnostics, and **find**, **awk**, and **tcpdump** for various administrative tasks. We learned to monitor processes with **ps**, **top**, and **htop**, start and terminate processes using **kill** and **pkill**, and adjust process priorities with **nice** and **renice**. Additionally, we managed background jobs with **bg** and **fg**, ensuring efficient multitasking.

In the section on package management, we covered the importance of maintaining up-to-date software using APT. We practiced updating package lists with **apt update**, upgrading software with **apt upgrade**, and installing packages like Git with **apt install**. Viewing and deleting packages with **dpkg** and **apt remove**, and finding packages with **apt search** were also demonstrated.

The chapter included managing system startup and shutdown processes using **shutdown**, **reboot**, and **systemctl** commands. We automated these tasks with **cron** and explored enabling Wake-on-LAN for remote startups. Managing specific services like Apache and MySQL using **systemctl** was learned, along with scheduling service restarts with **cron**.

Finally, accessing and using Linux utilities such as **cp**, **mv**, **grep**, **sed**, **awk**, **ping**, **traceroute**, **netstat**, **curl**, **top**, **df**, **du**, **tar**, **gzip**, **zip**, **fdisk**, and **lsblk** equipped us with tools for file management, text processing, network diagnostics, system monitoring, and disk management. This extensive chapter established a firm groundwork for administering Linux servers and efficiently managing our AlphaProject.

CHAPTER II: MANAGING LINUX SYSTEMS

Overview

This chapter will explore the fundamentals of Linux system administration, with an emphasis on the knowledge, abilities, and resources that are necessary for this role. The first step in making your Linux environment work for you is to learn how to navigate the system configuration files. By learning where these files are located, you'll be able to tweak the system's behavior and performance as needed.

Up next, you'll find out how to utilize systemd, a popular and capable system and service manager, to control system services. By learning how to start, stop, enable, and monitor services, you can keep your system running efficiently and in peak condition. In addition, you will learn the fundamentals of batch processing, crontab, and at, which are critical for automating regular operations and maintenance chores.

Another important topic covered in this chapter is monitoring the performance of the system. You will learn how to use different tools to monitor disk, memory, and CPU utilization, which will aid in finding and fixing performance issues. Log files and system logging are also covered, which are important for troubleshooting and keeping the system healthy. For a well-rounded understanding of how to operate Linux systems safely and efficiently, this chapter will also walk you through disk partitioning, system backup and restoration, and SSH remote administration.

Getting around System Configuration Files

A Linux system's behavior and interactions with hardware and software are dictated by its system configuration files, which are essential components of the system. From user permissions and network settings to service configurations and system security, these files manage it all. A successful system administrator must be familiar with the format and location of these files.

Characteristics of System Configuration Files

System configuration files are typically plain text files, making them easy to read and edit using any text editor like **`nano`**, **`vim`**, or **`gedit`**. They are usually stored in specific directories and are accessible only to users with appropriate permissions, often requiring superuser access to modify.

Configuration files can be divided into two main types:

- Global Configuration Files: These files affect the entire system and are located in **`/etc`**. Examples include **`/etc/passwd`** for user accounts and **`/etc/fstab`** for filesystem mounts.
- Local Configuration Files: These files affect individual users and are located in user-specific directories like **`/home/username`**. Examples include **`.bashrc`** for shell configuration and **`.gitconfig`** for Git settings.

Categories of Configuration Files

Configuration files can be categorized based on the services or components they manage. Following are some common categories:

1. System-Wide Configuration Files:
    - **/etc/passwd**: Contains user account information.
    - **/etc/group**: Defines groups of users.
    - **/etc/fstab**: Lists filesystems to be mounted at boot.
    - **/etc/hostname**: Defines the system's hostname.
    - **/etc/hosts**: Maps hostnames to IP addresses.
2. Network Configuration Files:
    - **/etc/network/interfaces** or **/etc/netplan/*.yaml**: Network interface configuration.
    - **/etc/resolv.conf**: DNS resolver configuration.
    - **/etc/hosts.allow** and **/etc/hosts.deny**: TCP wrappers configuration for access control.
3. Service Configuration Files:
    - **/etc/apache2/apache2.conf**: Apache web server configuration.
    - **/etc/mysql/my.cnf**: MySQL database configuration.
    - **/etc/ssh/sshd_config**: SSH server configuration.
4. Security Configuration Files:
    - **/etc/sudoers**: Sudo permissions configuration.
    - **/etc/selinux/config**: SELinux configuration.
    - **/etc/firewalld/firewalld.conf**: Firewall configuration.
5. Application Configuration Files:
    - **/etc/gitconfig**: System-wide Git configuration.
    - **/etc/php/7.4/apache2/php.ini**: PHP configuration for Apache.

Customizing Configuration Files

Customizing configuration files allows you to tailor the system and its services to meet specific needs. Given below is how you can approach customizing these files:

Editing Configuration Files

To edit a configuration file, you typically need superuser privileges. For example, to edit the SSH configuration file:

```
$ sudo nano /etc/ssh/sshd_config
```

After making changes, save the file and restart the service to apply the changes:

```
$ sudo systemctl restart sshd
```

Backup Configuration Files

Before editing a configuration file, it is wise to create a backup. This allows you to restore the original settings if something goes wrong:

```
$ sudo cp /etc/ssh/sshd_config /etc/ssh/sshd_config.bak
```

Understanding Configuration Syntax

Configuration files have specific syntax rules. For instance, **`sshd_config`** uses keyword-value pairs, while **`fstab`** uses a space-separated format. Incorrect syntax can prevent services from starting or cause errors, so be sure to understand the format before making changes.

Sample Program: Customizing Configuration Files

We shall walk through some examples relevant to AlphaProject:

Customizing Network Settings

Suppose you need to configure a static IP address for a network interface. On systems using **`netplan`**, you would edit the relevant YAML file in **`/etc/netplan/`**.

- Open the configuration file:

```
$ sudo nano /etc/netplan/01-netcfg.yaml
```

- Add the following configuration for a static IP:

```
network:
 version: 2
 ethernets:
 eth0:
 dhcp4: no
 addresses: [192.168.1.100/24]
 gateway4: 192.168.1.1
 nameservers:
 addresses: [8.8.8.8, 8.8.4.4]
```

- Apply the changes with:

```
$ sudo netplan apply
```

Configuring SSH

To enhance security, you might want to change the default SSH port and disable root login.

- Edit the SSH configuration file:

```
$ sudo nano /etc/ssh/sshd_config
```

- Change the following lines:

```
Port 2222
PermitRootLogin no
```

- Restart the SSH service:

```
$ sudo systemctl restart sshd
```

Setting up User Accounts

User accounts are managed in **/etc/passwd** and **/etc/shadow**. To manually add a user, you might edit these files directly, though using **useradd** is safer:

```
$ sudo useradd -m -s /bin/bash newuser

$ sudo passwd newuser
```

Configuring Apache Web Server

For the AlphaProject, you might need to configure Apache to host the project's website.

- Edit the main Apache configuration file:

```
$ sudo nano /etc/apache2/sites-available/000-default.conf
```

- Update the **DocumentRoot** to point to your project's directory:

```
DocumentRoot /projects/AlphaProject/public_html
```

- Enable the site and restart Apache:

```
$ sudo a2ensite 000-default.conf

$ sudo systemctl restart apache2
```

Managing Services

Service management often involves editing configuration files specific to the service. For example, to configure MySQL for AlphaProject,

- edit **/etc/mysql/my.cnf**:

```
$ sudo nano /etc/mysql/my.cnf
```

- Adjust settings such as the **bind-address** to allow remote connections:

```
bind-address = 0.0.0.0
```

- Restart the MySQL service:

```
$ sudo systemctl restart mysql
```

Configuring User and Group Permissions

The **/etc/sudoers** file controls sudo access. To allow a new user **newuser** to execute all commands, use **visudo** to edit this file safely:

```
$ sudo visudo
```

- Add the following line:

```
newuser ALL=(ALL) ALL
```

Setting System Locale

Locale settings can be configured in **/etc/default/locale**. To change the system language to US English:

```
$ sudo nano /etc/default/locale
```

- Add or modify the following lines:

```
LANG="en_US.UTF-8"
```

- Apply the locale changes:

```
$ sudo update-locale
```

Automating Configuration Changes

Scripts can automate the process of editing configuration files. For example, a script to configure network settings might look like this:

```
#!/bin/bash

cat <<EOL > /etc/netplan/01-netcfg.yaml
```

```
network:
 version: 2
 ethernets:
 eth0:
 dhcp4: no
 addresses: [192.168.1.100/24]
 gateway4: 192.168.1.1
 nameservers:
 addresses: [8.8.8.8, 8.8.4.4]
EOL
sudo netplan apply
```

The ability to diagnose problems, enhance performance, and guarantee system security is essential for any system manager, and this expertise is the bedrock of that profession. Your capacity to handle Linux systems effectively will be enhanced as we move further in this chapter and apply these skills to increasingly complicated and automated settings.

Managing System Services with 'systemd'

'systemd' Components

systemd is a modern system and service manager for Linux, designed to provide a robust and efficient way to manage system initialization, service control, and other critical functions. It has become the default init system on many Linux distributions, including Ubuntu, replacing older systems like System V init and Upstart.

To effectively use **systemd**, it is essential to understand its key components and how they interact:

1. Unit Files: These are configuration files that describe the state and behavior of services, sockets, devices, mounts, and more. Each unit file has a specific type, indicated by its

suffix, such as **.service** for services, **.socket** for sockets, and **.target** for target groups.

2. systemctl: This is the command-line tool used to interact with **systemd**. It allows you to start, stop, enable, disable, and monitor services and other units.
3. journalctl: This tool is used for querying and displaying logs collected by **systemd-journald**, the logging component of **systemd**.
4. Targets: Targets are special unit files that group other units together, providing a way to bring the system to a specific state. For example, **multi-user.target** is similar to runlevel 3 in System V init systems, providing a multi-user, non-graphical environment.

Managing System Services with systemd

systemd simplifies service management by providing consistent commands and functionality. We shall explore how to use **systemd** to manage system services practically, using examples relevant to our AlphaProject.

Viewing Service Status

To view the status of a specific service, use the **systemctl status** command followed by the service name. For instance, to check the status of the Apache web server:

```
$ sudo systemctl status apache2
```

This command displays detailed information about the service, including whether it is running, its PID, recent log entries, and more.

Starting and Stopping Services

To start a service, use the **systemctl start** command:

```
$ sudo systemctl start apache2
```

To stop a service, use the **systemctl stop** command:

```
$ sudo systemctl stop apache2
```

These commands ensure that the specified service starts or stops immediately.

Restarting and Reloading Services

If you need to restart a service (stop and then start it again), use the **systemctl restart** command:

```
$ sudo systemctl restart apache2
```

To reload a service's configuration without stopping it, use the **systemctl reload** command:

```
$ sudo systemctl reload apache2
```

Reloading is useful when changes have been made to a configuration file, and you want to apply them without disrupting the service.

Enabling and Disabling Services at Boot

To ensure a service starts automatically at boot, use the **systemctl enable** command:

```
$ sudo systemctl enable apache2
```

To prevent a service from starting at boot, use the **systemctl disable** command:

```
$ sudo systemctl disable apache2
```

These commands modify symbolic links in the appropriate directories to control whether a service is started automatically during the system's boot process.

Checking All Services

To view all active services, use:

```
$ systemctl list-units --type=service
```

For a complete list of all services, whether active or inactive, use:

```
$ systemctl list-units --type=service --all
```

Analyzing Boot Performance

systemd can help analyze the system's boot performance using the **systemd-analyze**

command. To view the overall boot time:

```
$ systemd-analyze
```

To get a detailed breakdown of time taken by each service during boot, use:

```
$ systemd-analyze blame
```

These commands help identify any services that are causing slow boot times.

Managing Dependencies

Services often have dependencies on other services. **systemd** manages these dependencies using **After=**, **Requires=**, and **Wants=** directives in unit files. For example, to ensure that a web application service starts after the database service, you would modify the unit file for the web application:

```
$ sudo nano /etc/systemd/system/webapp.service
```

Add the following lines:

```
[Unit]
Description=Web Application
After=mysql.service

[Service]
ExecStart=/usr/bin/webapp

[Install]
WantedBy=multi-user.target
```

Reload the systemd configuration to apply changes:

```
$ sudo systemctl daemon-reload
```

This configuration ensures the web application service starts after the MySQL service.

Creating Custom Service Units

Creating custom service units allows you to manage custom applications or scripts. Given below is how to create a custom service for a script used in AlphaProject:

- Create the Service File:

```
$ sudo nano /etc/systemd/system/alphaproject-backup.service
```

- Add Service Configuration:

```
[Unit]

Description=AlphaProject Backup Service



[Service]

ExecStart=/projects/AlphaProject/scripts/backup.sh

User=backupuser

Group=backupgroup



[Install]

WantedBy=multi-user.target
```

- Reload **systemd** Configuration:

```
$ sudo systemctl daemon-reload
```

- Start the Service:

```
$ sudo systemctl start alphaproject-backup
```

- Enable the Service at Boot:

```
$ sudo systemctl enable alphaproject-backup
```

Logging with journalctl

systemd uses **journald** for logging. You can access logs using **journalctl**. To view logs for a specific service:

```
$ sudo journalctl -u apache2
```

- To view the entire system journal:

```
$ sudo journalctl
```

- For real-time log updates:

```
$ sudo journalctl -f
```

Handling Service Failures

systemd provides mechanisms to handle service failures. For example, to automatically restart a service on failure, modify the service unit file:

```
$ sudo nano /etc/systemd/system/apache2.service
```

- Add the following under the **[Service]** section:

```
[Service]

Restart=on-failure
```

- Reload the configuration and restart the service:

```
$ sudo systemctl daemon-reload

$ sudo systemctl restart apache2
```

Sample Program: Using 'systemd' to Manage AlphaProject Services

For AlphaProject, suppose you need to manage an Apache web server and a MySQL database server. Given below is how you can use **systemd** to manage these services:

- Check Service Status:

```
$ sudo systemctl status apache2

$ sudo systemctl status mysql
```

- Start and Enable Services:

```
$ sudo systemctl start apache2

$ sudo systemctl enable apache2

$ sudo systemctl start mysql

$ sudo systemctl enable mysql
```

- Restart Services After Configuration Changes:

```
$ sudo systemctl restart apache2

$ sudo systemctl restart mysql
```

- Analyze Boot Performance:

```
$ systemd-analyze blame
```

- Monitor Logs:

```
$ sudo journalctl -u apache2
```

```
$ sudo journalctl -u mysql
```

- Configure Service Dependencies:

Edit the MySQL service unit file to ensure Apache starts after MySQL:

```
$ sudo nano /etc/systemd/system/apache2.service

[Unit]

Description=Apache Web Server

After=mysql.service
```

You can automate, monitor, and control services on your Linux system by learning components like journalctl, systemctl, and unit files. Your web and database servers will function efficiently, dependencies will be handled appropriately, and any difficulties will be rapidly recognized and remedied if you apply these abilities to manage AlphaProject's services.

Using 'crontab'

In Linux and other Unix-like operating systems, Cron is a tool for scheduling jobs depending on time. With its help, users can automate routine tasks and maintenance by setting scripts or commands to execute at predetermined intervals or times. System administrators can benefit greatly from Cron if they need to automate the execution of frequent activities.

Introduction to Cron Utility

The cron utility consists of the cron daemon (**crond**) and a set of configuration files known as **crontabs**. The daemon runs in the background and checks the **crontab** files for scheduled tasks, executing them at the specified times. Each user on the system can have their own **crontab**, and there is also a system-wide **crontab** for tasks that require elevated privileges.

Understanding crontab

A **crontab** file contains a list of cron jobs, each defined by a specific syntax that specifies when the job should run and what command should be executed. The basic structure of a **crontab** entry is as follows:

```
* * * * * command_to_execute
```

```
| | | | |

| | | | +---- Day of the week (0 - 7) (Sunday is both 0
and 7)

| | | +------ Month (1 - 12)

| | +-------- Day of the month (1 - 31)

| +---------- Hour (0 - 23)

+------------ Minute (0 - 59)
```

Each field can contain specific values, ranges, wildcards (*****), or step values (***/2** for every second unit).

To edit a user's **crontab**, you use the **crontab -e** command. This command opens the **crontab** file in the default text editor. To view the current **crontab**, use **crontab -l**, and to remove the current **crontab**, use **crontab -r**.

Sample Program: Using crontab in AlphaProject

We shall explore how to use **crontab** to automate various tasks for the AlphaProject. We'll set up jobs to perform regular backups, clean up temporary files, monitor system health, and more.

Setting up a Backup Job

Suppose you want to back up the AlphaProject directory to an external drive every night at midnight. First, create a backup script:

```
$ sudo nano /projects/AlphaProject/scripts/backup.sh
```

Add the following lines to the script:

```
#!/bin/bash

tar -czf /backup/AlphaProject_$(date +\%F).tar.gz
/projects/AlphaProject
```

Make the script executable:

```
$ sudo chmod +x /projects/AlphaProject/scripts/backup.sh
```

Now, schedule this script to run at midnight every day using **`crontab`**:

```
$ sudo crontab -e
```

Add the following line to the **`crontab`** file:

```
0 0 * * * /projects/AlphaProject/scripts/backup.sh
```

This cron job runs the backup script every day at midnight.

Cleaning up Temporary Files

To prevent disk space issues, you might want to delete temporary files older than a week from the **`tmp`** directory weekly. Create a cleanup script:

```
$ sudo nano /projects/AlphaProject/scripts/cleanup.sh
```

Add the following lines:

```
#!/bin/bash

find /projects/AlphaProject/tmp -type f -mtime +7 -exec
rm {} \;
```

Make the script executable:

```
$ sudo chmod +x /projects/AlphaProject/scripts/cleanup.sh
```

Schedule this script to run every Sunday at 2 AM:

```
$ sudo crontab -e
```

Add the following line:

```
0 2 * * 0 /projects/AlphaProject/scripts/cleanup.sh
```

Monitoring System Health

To monitor system health, you might want to log CPU and memory usage every hour. Create a monitoring script:

```
$ sudo nano /projects/AlphaProject/scripts/monitor.sh
```

Add the following lines:

```
#!/bin/bash

echo "$(date): CPU and Memory Usage" >>
/projects/AlphaProject/logs/system_health.log

top -b -n1 | grep "Cpu(s)" >>
/projects/AlphaProject/logs/system_health.log

free -m >> /projects/AlphaProject/logs/system_health.log
```

Make the script executable:

```
$ sudo chmod +x /projects/AlphaProject/scripts/monitor.sh
```

Schedule this script to run every hour:

```
$ sudo crontab -e
```

Add the following line:

```
0 * * * * /projects/AlphaProject/scripts/monitor.sh
```

Sending Email Notifications

You may want to receive an email notification if a critical service fails. First, ensure the **mail** command is available by installing the necessary package:

```
$ sudo apt install mailutils
```

Create a script to check the status of the Apache service and send an email if it is not running:

```
$ sudo nano
/projects/AlphaProject/scripts/check_apache.sh
```

Add the following lines:

```
#!/bin/bash

if ! systemctl is-active --quiet apache2; then

 echo "Apache service is down on $(hostname)" | mail -s
"Apache Service Alert" admin@gitforgits.com

fi
```

Make the script executable:

```
$ sudo chmod +x
/projects/AlphaProject/scripts/check_apache.sh
```

Schedule this script to run every 15 minutes:

```
$ sudo crontab -e
```

Add the following line:

```
*/15 * * * *
/projects/AlphaProject/scripts/check_apache.sh
```

Rotating Logs

Log files can grow quickly, consuming disk space. To rotate logs for the AlphaProject, create a log rotation script:

```
$ sudo nano /projects/AlphaProject/scripts/rotate_logs.sh
```

Add the following lines:

```
#!/bin/bash

logrotate /projects/AlphaProject/config/logrotate.conf
```

Create the logrotate configuration file:

```
$ sudo nano /projects/AlphaProject/config/logrotate.conf
```

Add the following configuration:

```
/projects/AlphaProject/logs/*.log {
 daily
 rotate 7
 compress
 missingok
 notifempty
 create 0640 root root
}
```

Make the script executable:

```
$ sudo chmod +x
/projects/AlphaProject/scripts/rotate_logs.sh
```

Schedule the log rotation script to run daily at 3 AM:

```
$ sudo crontab -e
```

Add the following line:

```
0 3 * * * /projects/AlphaProject/scripts/rotate_logs.sh
```

Custom Scheduling with Step Values

To run a script every 10 minutes, use step values in the **crontab** entry. For example, to check disk usage frequently:

```
$ sudo nano /projects/AlphaProject/scripts/check_disk.sh
```

Add the following lines:

```
#!/bin/bash

df -h > /projects/AlphaProject/logs/disk_usage.log
```

Make the script executable:

```
$ sudo chmod +x
/projects/AlphaProject/scripts/check_disk.sh
```

Schedule the script to run every 10 minutes:

```
$ sudo crontab -e
```

Add the following line:

```
*/10 * * * * /projects/AlphaProject/scripts/check_disk.sh
```

Viewing and Managing Cron Jobs

To view the list of scheduled cron jobs for the current user:

```
$ crontab -l
```

To remove all cron jobs for the current user:

```
$ crontab -r
```

If you need to edit the **crontab** for a different user (as the superuser):

```
$ sudo crontab -e -u username
```

To view the **crontab** for a different user:

```
$ sudo crontab -l -u username
```

One useful tool in Linux system administration is the ability to schedule and automate operations using crontab. You can automate a lot of tasks for AlphaProject, like backups, system monitoring, and log rotation, by learning how crontab entries are structured and using the cron program. In addition to assisting with system health and performance maintenance, these abilities automate routine maintenance, freeing up personnel for more important duties.

Scheduling Tasks with 'at' and 'batch'

In addition to **cron**, Linux provides **at** and **batch** utilities for scheduling tasks. Unlike **cron**, which is used for recurring tasks, **at** and **batch** are designed for one-time task scheduling. These commands offer a flexible way to execute jobs at a specific time or when system load permits, making them valuable tools for system administrators.

Introduction to 'at' and 'batch'

The **at** command is used to schedule a one-time task to run at a specific time in the future. The time can be specified in various formats, such as absolute time (e.g., **2:30 PM**), relative time (e.g., **now + 1 hour**), or specific dates (e.g., **midnight tomorrow**). The **at** daemon (**atd**) must be running for **at** jobs to be executed.

The **batch** command, on the other hand, schedules tasks to run when the system load average drops below a certain threshold, typically set to 1.5. This makes **batch** useful for executing non-urgent tasks during periods of low system activity, helping to maintain optimal performance.

Using at and batch in AlphaProject

The usage of at and batch to automate AlphaProject processes is something we should check out. We will plan out when to run scripts for routine maintenance, create reports, and create backups.

Scheduling One-Time Tasks with at

To use **at**, first ensure that the **at** package is installed and the **atd** daemon is running:

```
$ sudo apt install at
```

```
$ sudo systemctl start atd

$ sudo systemctl enable atd
```

Scheduling a Task

To schedule a task using **at**, enter the command followed by the desired execution time. For example, to schedule a script to run at 10:00 PM:

```
$ at 10:00 PM
```

After entering the command, you will be prompted to enter the command(s) you want to execute at the specified time. For example:

```
at> /projects/AlphaProject/scripts/maintenance.sh

at> <Ctrl+D> # Press Ctrl+D to save and exit
```

This schedules the **maintenance.sh** script to run at 10:00 PM.

Viewing Scheduled `at` Jobs

To view the list of scheduled **at** jobs, use the **atq** command:

```
$ atq
```

The output will display the job ID, execution time, and the user who scheduled the job.

Removing a Scheduled `at` Job

To remove a scheduled job, use the **atrm** command followed by the job ID:

```
$ atrm <job_id>
```

For example, to remove job ID 3:

```
$ atrm 3
```

Scheduling Tasks with Relative Time

You can also schedule tasks using relative time. For example, to run a script one hour from now:

```
$ at now + 1 hour
```

Enter the command to execute when prompted:

```
at> /projects/AlphaProject/scripts/report.sh

at> <Ctrl+D>
```

This schedules the **report.sh** script to run one hour from the current time.

Scheduling Tasks with Specific Dates

To schedule a task at a specific date and time, use the date format. For example, to run a script at midnight tomorrow:

```
$ at midnight tomorrow
```

Enter the command to execute when prompted:

```
at> /projects/AlphaProject/scripts/backup.sh

at> <Ctrl+D>
```

This schedules the **backup.sh** script to run at midnight the next day.

Using batch for System Load-Dependent Tasks

The **batch** command is useful for running tasks when the system load is low. This is particularly helpful for non-urgent tasks that should not interfere with system performance.

Scheduling a Task with `batch`

To schedule a task using **batch**, simply enter the **batch** command and then specify the command(s) to execute:

```
$ batch
```

Enter the command(s) to execute when prompted:

```
batch> /projects/AlphaProject/scripts/system_cleanup.sh
```

```
batch> <Ctrl+D>
```

This schedules the **system_cleanup.sh** script to run when the system load average drops below 1.5.

Viewing Scheduled batch Jobs

To view the list of scheduled **batch** jobs, use the same **atq** command:

```
$ atq
```

Batch jobs will be listed along with **at** jobs, distinguished by their queue identifiers.

Combining at and batch with Other Utilities

For complex workflows, you can combine **at** and **batch** with other utilities. For example, you might want to send an email notification after a task completes. Create a script that performs a task and sends an email:

```
$ sudo nano
/projects/AlphaProject/scripts/backup_and_notify.sh
```

Add the following lines:

```
#!/bin/bash

tar -czf /backup/AlphaProject_$(date +\%F).tar.gz
/projects/AlphaProject

echo "Backup completed on $(date)" | mail -s "Backup
Notification" admin@gitforgits.com
```

Make the script executable:

```
$ sudo chmod +x
/projects/AlphaProject/scripts/backup_and_notify.sh
```

Schedule the script to run at a specific time using **at**:

```
$ at 2:00 AM
```

Enter the command to execute when prompted:

```
at> /projects/AlphaProject/scripts/backup_and_notify.sh
at> <Ctrl+D>
```

This schedules the **backup_and_notify.sh** script to run at 2:00 AM, perform the backup, and send an email notification.

Automating System Health Checks

You can also use **at** to automate system health checks. Create a script that checks system health and logs the results:

```
$ sudo nano
/projects/AlphaProject/scripts/system_health_check.sh
```

Add the following lines:

```
#!/bin/bash

echo "$(date): System Health Check" >>
/projects/AlphaProject/logs/system_health.log

top -b -n1 | grep "Cpu(s)" >>
/projects/AlphaProject/logs/system_health.log

df -h >> /projects/AlphaProject/logs/system_health.log
```

Make the script executable:

```
$ sudo chmod +x
/projects/AlphaProject/scripts/system_health_check.sh
```

Schedule the script to run at a specific time using **at**:

```
$ at 6:00 AM
```

Enter the command to execute when prompted:

```
at> /projects/AlphaProject/scripts/system_health_check.sh

at> <Ctrl+D>
```

This schedules the **system_health_check.sh** script to run at 6:00 AM and log system health information.

Managing and Viewing Logs

Use **journalctl** to view logs related to **at** and **batch** jobs. For example, to view logs for **atd**:

```
$ sudo journalctl -u atd
```

This command displays log entries for the **atd** service, helping you troubleshoot any issues with scheduled tasks.

The at and batch commands offer versatile alternatives for organizing tasks that occur only once or depend on the system load. You can automate a lot of things for AlphaProject by learning and using these commands. You can run maintenance scripts, generate reports, back up your data, and check the system's health. You have a full range of options for automating system administration chores with these tools, which complement cron's recurring job scheduling features.

Monitoring System Performance

The effectiveness and efficiency of your Linux systems depend on your ability to monitor their performance. Finding slow spots, fixing problems, and keeping the system running smoothly are all benefits of good performance monitoring. Important metrics to track include processing power, memory, disk I/O, network traffic, and system health in general.

Key Metrics to Monitor

1. CPU Usage: High CPU usage can indicate processes that are consuming excessive resources, potentially impacting system performance.
2. Memory Usage: Monitoring memory usage helps in understanding how the system's RAM is being utilized and identifying potential memory leaks.

3. Disk I/O: Disk read/write operations can be a significant performance bottleneck, especially in I/O-intensive applications.
4. Network Activity: Monitoring network traffic is essential to ensure that the network bandwidth is sufficient and that there are no unexpected spikes in usage.
5. System Load: The load average provides a snapshot of the system's workload over time, helping to gauge overall system performance.

System Performance Monitoring Tools

Various tools are available for monitoring different aspects of system performance. We shall explore these tools and how to use them practically for AlphaProject.

'top'

The **top** command provides a dynamic, real-time view of system processes and resource usage. It displays information such as CPU usage, memory usage, and load averages.

To use **top**, simply type:

```
$ top
```

This command opens an interactive interface where you can see which processes are consuming the most resources. Press **q** to exit.

'vnstat'

vnstat is a network traffic monitor that tracks and logs network bandwidth usage. To install **vnstat**:

```
$ sudo apt install vnstat
```

To initialize the database for a specific interface (e.g., **eth0**):

```
$ sudo vnstat -u -i eth0

$ sudo systemctl start vnstat

$ sudo systemctl enable vnstat
```

To view network statistics:

```
$ vnstat
```

This command displays the network traffic statistics for the specified interface.

'nagios'

Nagios is a powerful monitoring system that can track the status of network services, host resources, and other network elements. To set up **Nagios**, follow these steps:

First, install **Nagios** and its plugins:

```
$ sudo apt install nagios3 nagios-plugins
```

Start the Nagios service:

```
$ sudo systemctl start nagios3

$ sudo systemctl enable nagios3
```

To access the Nagios web interface, navigate to **http://<your-server-ip>/nagios3** in a web browser. Use the default credentials to log in. From the web interface, you can configure various services and hosts to be monitored.

'iftop'

iftop is a real-time network bandwidth monitoring tool. It shows a list of network connections from/to your system and their data transfer rates.

To install **iftop**:

```
$ sudo apt install iftop
```

Run **iftop** with:

```
$ sudo iftop
```

This command opens an interactive interface displaying real-time bandwidth usage. Press **q** to exit.

'psacct'

psacct (Process Accounting) tracks and reports on the resource usage of individual processes. To install **psacct**:

```
$ sudo apt install acct
```

Start the accounting service:

```
$ sudo systemctl start acct

$ sudo systemctl enable acct
```

To display the resource usage of all commands executed by users:

```
$ sa
```

To display a summary of commands executed by a specific user:

```
$ sa -u username
```

To view the details of individual commands executed:

```
$ ac -d
```

'iostat'

iostat is part of the **sysstat** package and provides statistics on CPU and I/O usage. To install **sysstat**:

```
$ sudo apt install sysstat
```

To display CPU and I/O statistics:

```
$ iostat
```

This command provides a report on CPU utilization and I/O statistics for devices.

'netstat'

netstat displays network connections, routing tables, interface statistics, masquerade connections, and multicast memberships.

To display all active connections and listening ports:

```
$ netstat -tuln
```

To view network statistics:

```
$ netstat -s
```

To continuously monitor network connections, use:

```
$ watch netstat -tuln
```

Sample Program: Monitoring Tools in AlphaProject

We shall apply these monitoring tools to manage and monitor the AlphaProject system effectively.

Monitoring CPU and Memory Usage

Using **top** to monitor CPU and memory usage in real-time:

```
$ top
```

This helps identify processes that are consuming excessive resources. For a more user-friendly interface, you can use **htop**:

```
$ sudo apt install htop

$ htop
```

htop provides an interactive interface for monitoring system performance.

Tracking Network Traffic

Using **vnstat** to monitor network traffic on the **eth0** interface:

```
$ vnstat -i eth0
```

To get a detailed report:

```
$ vnstat -d
```

This command displays daily network traffic statistics.

Comprehensive System Monitoring with Nagios

Configure **Nagios** to monitor critical services like Apache and MySQL for AlphaProject. Edit the Nagios configuration file to add these services:

```
$ sudo nano /etc/nagios3/conf.d/localhost_nagios2.cfg
```

Add checks for Apache and MySQL:

```
define service {

 use generic-service

 host_name localhost

 service_description HTTP

 check_command check_http

}


define service {

 use generic-service

 host_name localhost

 service_description MySQL

 check_command check_mysql

}
```

Restart the Nagios service to apply changes:

```
$ sudo systemctl restart nagios3
```

Access the Nagios web interface to view the status of these services.

Real-Time Network Monitoring with iftop

Use **iftop** to monitor real-time bandwidth usage:

```
$ sudo iftop -i eth0
```

This command displays network connections and their data transfer rates.

Detailed Process Accounting with psacct

Using **psacct** to track resource usage of processes:

```
$ sa
```

To view the resource usage summary for a specific user:

```
$ sa -u username
```

This helps in understanding which users are consuming the most resources.

Disk and I/O Statistics with iostat

Using **iostat** to monitor disk and I/O statistics:

```
$ iostat -x 5
```

This command provides extended I/O statistics every 5 seconds, helping to identify I/O bottlenecks.

Network Connections and Statistics with netstat

Using **netstat** to display network connections:

```
$ netstat -tuln
```

To view network statistics:

```
$ netstat -s
```

This helps in monitoring active network connections and network traffic.

These tools are great for finding problems, making sure AlphaProject is running well, and avoiding bottlenecks. The more you use these monitoring tools, the more you'll be able to control and maintain your systems, making sure they function properly and efficiently.

Log Files and System Logging

In Linux, almost everything can be logged, including system events, application activity, user actions, and network traffic. Effective logging allows administrators to monitor system health, detect anomalies, and maintain audit trails.

What Can Be Logged in Linux

Various components generate logs, including:

1. System Logs: Logs generated by the operating system kernel and system services.
2. Application Logs: Logs generated by applications and services such as Apache, MySQL, and others.
3. Security Logs: Logs related to authentication, user actions, and security events.
4. Network Logs: Logs related to network activity and traffic.
5. Hardware Logs: Logs related to hardware events and performance.

Logging in Linux is achieved through various mechanisms, primarily using the **`syslog`** protocol. The **`syslog`** protocol is widely used for forwarding log messages in an IP network. Linux systems use syslog daemons like **`rsyslog`** or **`syslog-ng`** to handle logging.

Understanding Syslogs

Syslogs are a standard for message logging. They provide a centralized way to collect and manage logs from different sources. Syslogs categorize messages into facilities and severity levels, which help in organizing and filtering logs.

- Facilities: Represent different system components, such as **`auth`**, **`cron`**, **`daemon`**, **`kern`**, **`mail`**, **`user`**, etc.
- Severity Levels: Indicate the importance of the log message, ranging from **`emerg`**

(emergency) to **debug**.

Managing Syslogs with rsyslog

rsyslog is a powerful and flexible syslog daemon that extends the traditional syslog with additional features like reliable transport, filtering, and log rotation.

Installing and Configuring rsyslog

rsyslog is typically pre-installed on most Linux distributions. If it is not installed, you can install it using:

```
$ sudo apt install rsyslog
```

Ensure the **rsyslog** service is running:

```
$ sudo systemctl start rsyslog

$ sudo systemctl enable rsyslog
```

Understanding the rsyslog Configuration

The main configuration file for **rsyslog** is located at **/etc/rsyslog.conf**. This file controls the behavior of the logging system, including where logs are stored and how they are handled. Additional configuration files are often found in **/etc/rsyslog.d/**.

Basic Configuration Example

Given below is a simple program to understand the **rsyslog** configuration. Open the main configuration file:

```
$ sudo nano /etc/rsyslog.conf
```

To log all authentication messages to a separate file, add the following line:

```
auth.* /var/log/auth.log
```

This directive tells **rsyslog** to log all messages from the **auth** facility (regardless of severity) to **/var/log/auth.log**.

Customizing System Logs for AlphaProject

For AlphaProject, you might want to log application-specific messages to a dedicated file. Suppose you have a custom application logging messages to syslog using the **local0** facility. You can direct these logs to a separate file.

Add the following line to **/etc/rsyslog.conf**:

```
local0.* /var/log/alphaproject.log
```

Restart the **rsyslog** service to apply the changes:

```
$ sudo systemctl restart rsyslog
```

Accessing and Analyzing Logs

Logs are typically stored in the **/var/log** directory. Some common log files include:

- **/var/log/syslog**: General system log
- **/var/log/auth.log**: Authentication log
- **/var/log/kern.log**: Kernel log
- **/var/log/apache2**: Apache web server logs
- **/var/log/mysql**: MySQL logs

To view log files, you can use commands like **cat**, **less**, **tail**, and **grep**.

For example, to view the latest entries in the syslog:

```
$ tail -f /var/log/syslog
```

To search for specific entries, use **grep**:

```
$ grep "error" /var/log/syslog
```

Setting up Log Rotation

Log rotation is essential to manage log file sizes and ensure they don't consume excessive disk space. **logrotate** is a tool that automates log rotation, compression, and removal.

The main configuration file for **logrotate** is **/etc/logrotate.conf**, and additional configurations are in **/etc/logrotate.d/**.

Given below is an example of configuring log rotation for AlphaProject logs:

Create a configuration file:

```
$ sudo nano /etc/logrotate.d/alphaproject
```

Add the following configuration:

```
/var/log/alphaproject.log {
 daily
 rotate 7
 compress
 missingok
 notifempty
 create 0640 root root
 postrotate
 /usr/bin/systemctl reload rsyslog > /dev/null
 endscript
}
```

This configuration rotates the **alphaproject.log** file daily, keeps seven days of logs, compresses old logs, and ensures the log file is recreated with the correct permissions.

Remote Logging

For centralized log management, you might want to forward logs from multiple systems to a central log server. This is useful for large deployments like AlphaProject.

To configure remote logging, edit the **rsyslog** configuration file on the client systems:

```
$ sudo nano /etc/rsyslog.conf
```

Add the following line to forward logs to a remote server:

```
*.* @logserver.gitforgits.com:514
```

On the log server, configure **rsyslog** to receive logs. Open the configuration file:

```
$ sudo nano /etc/rsyslog.conf
```

Uncomment or add the following lines to enable TCP/UDP reception:

```
module(load="imtcp")

input(type="imtcp" port="514")


module(load="imudp")

input(type="imudp" port="514")
```

Restart **rsyslog** on both the client and server:

```
$ sudo systemctl restart rsyslog
```

Monitoring Logs with Logwatch

Logwatch is a log analysis tool that summarizes and reports log entries. To install **Logwatch**:

```
$ sudo apt install logwatch
```

To generate a report, use:

```
$ sudo logwatch --detail high --mailto
admin@gitforgits.com --range today
```

This command generates a detailed log report for today and emails it to **admin@gitforgits.com**.

Sample Program: Logging Messages

Custom Application Logging

Suppose AlphaProject has a custom application that logs messages to syslog using **local0**. Configure **rsyslog** to log these messages to a dedicated file:

```
$ sudo nano /etc/rsyslog.conf
```

Add:

```
local0.* /var/log/alphaproject.log
```

Restart **rsyslog**:

```
$ sudo systemctl restart rsyslog
```

Log Rotation for Application Logs

Ensure the logs for the custom application are rotated to prevent excessive disk usage:

```
$ sudo nano /etc/logrotate.d/alphaproject
```

Add:

```
/var/log/alphaproject.log {

 daily

 rotate 7

 compress

 missingok

 notifempty

 create 0640 root root
```

```
 postrotate
 /usr/bin/systemctl reload rsyslog > /dev/null
 endscript
}
```

Remote Logging Setup

Configure AlphaProject systems to forward logs to a central server:

On the client systems:

```
$ sudo nano /etc/rsyslog.conf
```

Add:

```
*.* @logserver.gitforgits.com:514
```

On the log server:

```
$ sudo nano /etc/rsyslog.conf
```

Enable TCP/UDP reception:

```
module(load="imtcp")
input(type="imtcp" port="514")

module(load="imudp")
input(type="imudp" port="514")
```

Restart **rsyslog**:

```
$ sudo systemctl restart rsyslog
```

Monitoring Logs with Logwatch:

Set up **Logwatch** to send daily summaries of log activity:

```
$ sudo logwatch --detail high --mailto
admin@gitforgits.com --range today
```

These practices help in detecting issues early, maintaining compliance, and optimizing system performance, thus ensuring the smooth operation of your systems.

Backing up and Restoring Systems

'rsync'

rsync stands for "remote sync" and is commonly used for backups, mirroring, and as an improved copy command for everyday use. It only transfers the differences between source and destination, making it highly efficient. It supports a range of options to control file permissions, compression, and recursive operations.

Key Features of rsync

- Delta Transfer Algorithm: Transfers only the changed parts of files.
- Compression: Reduces the amount of data sent over the network.
- Preserve Permissions and Ownership: Maintains file permissions, ownership, and timestamps.
- Versatile: Can be used for local and remote transfers.
- Bandwidth Limiting: Allows controlling the bandwidth used for the transfer.

Using rsync for AlphaProject

We shall explore how to use **rsync** to back up and restore the AlphaProject directory. We will set up a backup routine that copies project files to an external storage device and demonstrate restoring these files.

Installing rsync

rsync is usually pre-installed on most Linux distributions. If it is not installed, you can install it using:

```
$ sudo apt install rsync
```

Backing up Data with rsync

To back up the AlphaProject directory to an external drive mounted at **/mnt/backup**, use the following command:

```
$ rsync -avh /projects/AlphaProject /mnt/backup/
```

We shall break down the options used:

- **-a**: Archive mode, which preserves permissions, timestamps, symbolic links, and recursive copy.
- **-v**: Verbose mode, which displays detailed information during the transfer.
- **-h**: Human-readable format, making file sizes easier to read.

This command synchronizes the contents of **/projects/AlphaProject** to **/mnt/backup/AlphaProject**.

Scheduling Backups with cron

To automate the backup process, you can schedule it using **cron**. Edit the **crontab** file:

```
$ sudo crontab -e
```

Add the following line to schedule a backup every day at 2 AM:

```
0 2 * * * rsync -avh /projects/AlphaProject /mnt/backup/
```

Incremental Backups with rsync

For more efficient backups, you can use **rsync** to create incremental backups. This means only the changes since the last backup will be copied. To set up incremental backups, create a backup directory with date stamps:

```
$ rsync -avh --link-dest=/mnt/backup/AlphaProject-
previous /projects/AlphaProject /mnt/backup/AlphaProject-
$(date +\%F)
```

In this command:

- **--link-dest**: Uses hard links to avoid copying unchanged files, pointing to the previous backup.

You can update the **crontab** entry to perform this operation daily:

```
0 2 * * * rsync -avh --link-
dest=/mnt/backup/AlphaProject-previous
/projects/AlphaProject /mnt/backup/AlphaProject-$(date
+\%F)
```

Restoring Data with rsync

To restore data from the backup location to the original directory, use:

```
$ rsync -avh /mnt/backup/AlphaProject-YYYY-MM-DD/
/projects/AlphaProject/
```

Replace **YYYY-MM-DD** with the date of the backup you want to restore.

Verifying Backups

After performing backups, it is essential to verify them to ensure data integrity. You can use the **--checksum** option with **rsync** to verify the files:

```
$ rsync -avh --checksum /projects/AlphaProject
/mnt/backup/AlphaProject
```

This option compares files based on their checksums, ensuring that the files are identical.

Advanced 'rsync' Options

rsync offers several advanced options to customize your backup and restore processes:

Exclude Files

To exclude specific files or directories from the backup, use the **--exclude** option:

```
$ rsync -avh --exclude 'tmp/' /projects/AlphaProject
/mnt/backup/
```

This excludes the **tmp** directory from the backup.

Compression

To reduce the amount of data transferred, use the **-z** option for compression:

```
$ rsync -avhz /projects/AlphaProject /mnt/backup/
```

Bandwidth Limiting

To limit the bandwidth used by **rsync**, use the **--bwlimit** option:

```
$ rsync -avh --bwlimit=1000 /projects/AlphaProject
/mnt/backup/
```

This limits the transfer rate to 1000 KB/s.

Sample Program: Complete Backup and Restore Script

You can create a script that handles both backup and restore operations. Create a script file:

```
$ sudo nano
/projects/AlphaProject/scripts/backup_restore.sh
```

Add the following lines:

```
#!/bin/bash



BACKUP_DIR="/mnt/backup"

SOURCE_DIR="/projects/AlphaProject"

DATE=$(date +\%F)
```

```
LINK_DEST="$BACKUP_DIR/AlphaProject-previous"

# Backup Function
backup() {
 echo "Starting backup..."
 rsync -avh --link-dest=$LINK_DEST $SOURCE_DIR
$BACKUP_DIR/AlphaProject-$DATE
 echo "Backup completed."
}

# Restore Function
restore() {
 if [ -z "$1" ]; then
 echo "Please provide the backup date (YYYY-MM-DD) to
restore."
 exit 1
 fi
 echo "Starting restore from $1..."
 rsync -avh $BACKUP_DIR/AlphaProject-$1/ $SOURCE_DIR/
 echo "Restore completed."
}
```

```
# Main Script
case "$1" in
 backup)
 backup
 ;;
 restore)
 restore $2
 ;;
 *)
 echo "Usage: $0 {backup|restore YYYY-MM-DD}"
 exit 1
 ;;
esac
```

Make the script executable:

```
$ sudo chmod +x
/projects/AlphaProject/scripts/backup_restore.sh
```

To perform a backup, run:

```
$ /projects/AlphaProject/scripts/backup_restore.sh backup
```

To restore from a specific backup date, run:

```
$ /projects/AlphaProject/scripts/backup_restore.sh
restore YYYY-MM-DD
```

Relying on rsync for backup and restoration operations offers a strong and effective way to handle data in Linux. You can guarantee the availability and integrity of your AlphaProject data by setting up frequent backups, doing incremental backups, and making use of advanced customization options.

Perform Disk Partitioning

In Linux, disk partitioning can be performed using various tools such as **fdisk**, **parted**, and **gparted**. There are specific applications and benefits to using each tool. We'll take a look at these tools and show you how to partition the AlphaProject system in several ways.

Using 'fdisk'

fdisk is a command-line utility for managing disk partitions. It supports MBR (Master Boot Record) and GPT (GUID Partition Table) partitioning schemes.

Creating a New Partition with fdisk

- List Available Disks:

```
$ sudo fdisk -l
```

Identify the disk you want to partition, such as **/dev/sda**.

- Start **fdisk**:

```
$ sudo fdisk /dev/sda
```

This command opens the **fdisk** utility for the specified disk.

- Create a New Partition:
    - Type **n** to create a new partition.
    - Select the partition type (primary or extended). Typically, you choose **p** for primary.
    - Specify the partition number, starting and ending sectors. For simplicity, you can accept the default values to use the available space.
- Write Changes to Disk:

  Type **w** to write the changes and exit **fdisk**.

For example:

```
$ sudo fdisk /dev/sda

Command (m for help): n

Partition type

 p primary (1 primary, 0 extended, 3 free)

 e extended (container for logical partitions)

Select (default p): p

Partition number (2-4, default 2): 2

First sector (2048-20971519, default 2048): 4096

Last sector, +sectors or +size{K,M,G,T,P} (4096-20971519,
default 20971519): +1G


Command (m for help): w
```

- Format the Partition:

```
$ sudo mkfs.ext4 /dev/sda2
```

This formats the new partition with the ext4 filesystem.

- Mount the Partition:

```
$ sudo mkdir /mnt/new_partition

$ sudo mount /dev/sda2 /mnt/new_partition
```

Using 'parted'

parted is another command-line utility that supports both MBR and GPT partitioning schemes. It is more powerful and flexible than **fdisk**.

Creating a New Partition with parted

- Start **parted**:

```
$ sudo parted /dev/sda
```

This opens the **parted** utility for the specified disk.

- Set the Partition Table:

```
(parted) mklabel gpt
```

This command sets the partition table to GPT.

- Create a New Partition:

```
(parted) mkpart primary ext4 1MiB 2GiB
```

This creates a primary partition with the ext4 filesystem starting at 1MiB and ending at 2GiB.

- Print the Partition Table:

```
(parted) print
```

This command displays the partition layout.

- Quit **parted**:

```
(parted) quit
```

- Format the Partition:

```
$ sudo mkfs.ext4 /dev/sda1
```

- Mount the Partition:

```
$ sudo mkdir /mnt/new_partition

$ sudo mount /dev/sda1 /mnt/new_partition
```

Using 'gparted'

gparted is a graphical user interface (GUI) tool for managing disk partitions. It is useful for users who prefer a visual approach.

Creating a New Partition with gparted

- Install **gparted**:

```
$ sudo apt install gparted
```

- Launch **gparted**:

```
$ sudo gparted
```

This command opens the **gparted** GUI.

- Select the Disk:

Use the dropdown menu in the top-right corner to select the disk you want to partition, such as **/dev/sda**.

- Create a New Partition:
    - Click on the unallocated space.
    - Click the **New** button.
    - Set the partition size, filesystem type (e.g., ext4), and other options.
    - Click **Add** to create the partition.
    - Apply Changes:

Click the **Apply** button (green checkmark) to write the changes to the disk.

- Mount the Partition:

```
$ sudo mkdir /mnt/new_partition

$ sudo mount /dev/sda1 /mnt/new_partition
```

Creating a Swap Partition

A swap partition is used for extending the system's physical memory by using disk space.

- Using **fdisk** to Create a Swap Partition:

```
$ sudo fdisk /dev/sda

Command (m for help): n

Partition type

 p primary (1 primary, 0 extended, 3 free)

 e extended (container for logical partitions)

Select (default p): p

Partition number (2-4, default 2): 3

First sector (2048-20971519, default 2048): 20971520

Last sector, +sectors or +size{K,M,G,T,P} (20971520-
41943039, default 41943039): +1G


Command (m for help): t

Partition number (1-4, default 4): 3

Hex code (type L to list all codes): 82

Changed type of partition 'Linux' to 'Linux swap'.


Command (m for help): w
```

- Format and Enable Swap:

```
$ sudo mkswap /dev/sda3

$ sudo swapon /dev/sda3
```

- Add Swap to **/etc/fstab**:

```
$ sudo nano /etc/fstab
```

- Add the following line:

```
/dev/sda3 none swap sw 0 0
```

Resizing Partitions with parted

You may need to resize partitions to allocate more space for a specific partition.

- Resize a Partition with **parted**:

```
$ sudo parted /dev/sda

(parted) resizepart 1 3GiB
```

- Resize Filesystem:

```
$ sudo resize2fs /dev/sda1
```

Creating Logical Volumes with LVM

Logical Volume Manager (LVM) allows flexible disk management.

- Install LVM Tools:

```
$ sudo apt install lvm2
```

- Create Physical Volume:

```
$ sudo pvcreate /dev/sda2
```

- Create Volume Group:

```
$ sudo vgcreate vg_alpha /dev/sda2
```

- Create Logical Volume:

```
$ sudo lvcreate -L 1G -n lv_alpha vg_alpha
```

- Format and Mount Logical Volume:

```
$ sudo mkfs.ext4 /dev/vg_alpha/lv_alpha

$ sudo mkdir /mnt/lv_alpha

$ sudo mount /dev/vg_alpha/lv_alpha /mnt/lv_alpha
```

With a good grasp of these tools, from command-line flexibility to graphical simplicity, you can efficiently manage partitions for AlphaProject, including creating, resizing, and setting up swap space, as well as advanced techniques like LVM.

Using SSH for Remote Management

When working with distant computers over an insecure network, it is important to use a protocol like Secure Shell (SSH). Secure Shell (SSH) is an essential tool for system administrators since it allows for encrypted communication sessions. It enables safe remote login, file transfer, and command execution.

Setting up SSH

To use SSH, you need an SSH server running on the remote machine and an SSH client on the local machine. Most Linux distributions come with **OpenSSH** installed by default. If it is not installed, you can install it using the following commands.

Installing SSH Server

On the remote machine:

```
$ sudo apt install openssh-server
```

Start and enable the SSH server:

```
$ sudo systemctl start ssh

$ sudo systemctl enable ssh
```

Installing SSH Client

On the local machine:

```
$ sudo apt install openssh-client
```

Connecting to a Remote System

To connect to a remote system, you need the IP address or hostname of the remote machine and the login credentials. The basic syntax of the SSH command is:

```
$ ssh username@hostname
```

For example, to connect to a remote server with IP address **192.168.1.100** and username **user**:

```
$ ssh user@192.168.1.100
```

Key-Based Authentication

Key-based authentication is more secure than password-based authentication. It uses a pair of cryptographic keys: a private key stored on your local machine and a public key stored on the remote machine.

Generating SSH Keys

On the local machine:

```
$ ssh-keygen -t rsa -b 4096 -C
"your_email@gitforgits.com"
```

This command generates a public-private key pair. By default, the keys are stored in **~/.ssh/id_rsa** (private key) and **~/.ssh/id_rsa.pub** (public key).

Copying the Public Key to the Remote Machine

Use **ssh-copy-id** to copy the public key to the remote machine:

```
$ ssh-copy-id user@192.168.1.100
```

You will be prompted to enter the remote user's password. After the key is copied, you can log in without a password.

Manually Adding the Public Key

Alternatively, you can manually add the public key to the **~/.ssh/authorized_keys** file on the remote machine:

```
$ cat ~/.ssh/id_rsa.pub | ssh user@192.168.1.100 'cat >>
~/.ssh/authorized_keys'
```

SSH Config File

You can simplify SSH connections using the SSH config file located at **~/.ssh/config**. This file allows you to create shortcuts for your SSH connections.

Creating an SSH Config File

Open the SSH config file:

```
$ nano ~/.ssh/config
```

Add the following configuration:

```
Host alpha

 HostName 192.168.1.100

 User user

 IdentityFile ~/.ssh/id_rsa
```

Now you can connect to the remote server using the shortcut:

```
$ ssh alpha
```

Port Forwarding

SSH allows port forwarding, which can be used to securely tunnel network connections. There are two types of port forwarding: local and remote.

Local Port Forwarding

Local port forwarding forwards traffic from a local port to a remote server. For example, to forward local port **8080** to **gitforgits.com** on port **80**:

```
$ ssh -L 8080:gitforgits.com:80 user@192.168.1.100
```

Access **http://localhost:8080** on your local machine to reach **gitforgits.com**.

Remote Port Forwarding

Remote port forwarding forwards traffic from a remote port to a local server. For example, to forward remote port **9090** on the remote server to local port **3000**:

```
$ ssh -R 9090:localhost:3000 user@192.168.1.100
```

Access **http://remote-server:9090** to reach **http://localhost:3000** on your local machine.

Copying Files using scp and rsync

SSH allows secure file transfer between local and remote systems using **scp** and **rsync**.

Using 'scp'

The **scp** (secure copy) command copies files between local and remote systems. To copy a file from your local machine to the remote machine:

```
$ scp localfile.txt user@192.168.1.100:/remote/directory/
```

To copy a file from the remote machine to your local machine:

```
$ scp user@192.168.1.100:/remote/file.txt
/local/directory/
```

Using 'rsync'

rsync is a powerful tool for synchronizing files between local and remote systems. To sync a local directory to a remote directory:

```
$ rsync -avh /local/directory/
user@192.168.1.100:/remote/directory/
```

To sync a remote directory to a local directory:

```
$ rsync -avh user@192.168.1.100:/remote/directory/
/local/directory/
```

Executing Commands on a Remote System

You can execute commands on a remote system directly from your local machine using SSH. For example, to check the disk usage on the remote machine:

```
$ ssh user@192.168.1.100 'df -h'
```

To update the package list on the remote machine:

```
$ ssh user@192.168.1.100 'sudo apt update'
```

Using tmux with SSH

tmux is a terminal multiplexer that allows you to manage multiple terminal sessions within a single window. It is particularly useful for maintaining long-running processes over SSH sessions.

- Installing **tmux**:

```
$ sudo apt install tmux
```

- Starting a **tmux** Session:

```
$ tmux new -s session_name
```

Within the **tmux** session, you can start multiple windows and panes.

- Detaching and Reattaching to **tmux** Sessions:

To detach from a **tmux** session:

```
<Ctrl-b> d
```

To reattach to the session:

```
$ tmux attach -t session_name
```

Managing Multiple Servers with SSH

You can use tools like **cssh** (Cluster SSH) or **tmux** to manage multiple servers simultaneously.

Using 'cssh'

cssh opens an SSH session to multiple servers and allows you to send commands to all sessions simultaneously.

Using **tmux** with Multiple SSH Sessions

You can open multiple panes in **tmux**, each connected to a different server. To split the current pane horizontally:

```
<Ctrl-b> "
```

To split the current pane vertically:

```
<Ctrl-b> %
```

To navigate between panes:

```
<Ctrl-b> arrow_key
```

Monitoring Remote Systems with top and htop

You can use **top** and **htop** to monitor system performance on remote systems over SSH.

Using 'top'

```
$ ssh user@192.168.1.100 'top'
```

Using 'htop'

First, install **htop** on the remote system:

```
$ sudo apt install htop
```

Then, run **htop** over SSH:

```
$ ssh user@192.168.1.100 'htop'
```

Through the utilization of Secure Shell (SSH) for remote management, it is possible to manage, monitor, and maintain remote systems in a secure and efficient manner, hence guaranteeing the highest possible level of performance and dependability for Alpha project.

Summary

We explored the fundamentals of Linux system administration in this chapter, with an emphasis on the practical skills necessary for good system management. The first step was to familiarize ourselves with system configuration files, their features, and how to make changes to them. To better control system services, we dove into systemd, learning its parts and how to use its commands. The use of systemctl for initiating, terminating, enabling, and monitoring services was part of this. The crontab utility was the next thing we looked at, and we learned how to automate backups, schedule recurring jobs, and do system maintenance with it. After that, we used the at command to schedule one-time tasks and the batch command for jobs that depend on the current load.

Top, vnstat, nagios, iftop, psacct, iostat, and netstat are just a few of the tools for system performance monitoring that we covered in this chapter. You might learn about the system's memory, CPU, disk I/O, network activity, and general health with these tools. We also went over system logging, including what information may be recorded and how to set up rsyslog to collect all of that data in one place. This involved making changes to the log files, use logrotate to set up log rotation, then analyzing logs with logwatch.

We looked at rsync as a backup and restore tool, automated and incremental backup configuration, and data integrity assurance. Furthermore, we used disk partitioning programs such as fdisk, parted, and gparted to create and resize partitions, as well as set up logical volumes with LVM. Our further understanding of Secure Shell (SSH) for remote administration concluded with topics such as key-based authentication, SSH configuration files, port forwarding, scp and rsync secure file transfers, and the use of tmux to handle numerous SSH sessions. These all-encompassing abilities are vital for keeping Linux systems running smoothly and efficiently in every setting.

CHAPTER III: UPGRADING, INSTALLING, AND CONFIGURING SOFTWARE AND HARDWARE

Overview

Upgrading, installing, and configuring Linux hardware and software are the primary topics covered in this chapter. This chapter will teach you how to use apt, the main package management tool for Debian-based distributions, and yum, the primary package management tool for Red Hat-based distributions. These tools will make program installation, updating, and removal effortless. We will also go over the basics of dependency management, which is making sure that your apps can't function properly without certain libraries and components.

This chapter also covers another crucial part, which is configuring the system hardware. You'll be able to manage different hardware components, update the kernel, and work with device drivers. You will be able to optimize hardware performance and resolve hardware-related problems with this information. For software package acquisition and update management, we will also cover repository setup and management.

In addition, the concepts of virtualization and containerization will be introduced in this chapter. You will get the hang of using VirtualBox to set up and manage virtual machines, which will allow you to install and run various OSes on a single physical computer.

Package Management with 'apt'

In order to successfully install, update, and delete software packages, package management is a vital part of Linux system maintenance. Two of the most widely used package managers in the Linux world are **apt** (Advanced Package Tool) for Debian-based distributions like Ubuntu, and **yum** (Yellowdog Updater Modified) for Red Hat-based distributions like CentOS and Fedora.

Introduction to 'apt' and 'yum'

'apt' (Advanced Package Tool)

- Debian-Based Distributions: Used primarily in Debian, Ubuntu, and their derivatives.
- Functionality: Simplifies the process of managing software by handling dependencies, fetching packages from repositories, and keeping the system up-to-date.
- Common Commands: **apt-get**, **apt-cache**, **apt**.

'yum' (Yellowdog Updater Modified)

- Red Hat-Based Distributions: Used in Red Hat Enterprise Linux, CentOS, Fedora, and their derivatives.
- Functionality: Manages RPM packages, resolves dependencies, and handles package installations and updates.

- Common Commands: **yum**, **yum-config-manager**, **yum-repolist**.

Installing 'apt' in Our Existing Environment

Assuming our environment is Ubuntu-based (since **apt** is the default package manager here), **apt** should already be installed. If it isn't, you can install it by ensuring your system has **apt**:

```
$ sudo apt update

$ sudo apt install apt
```

This command updates the package list and installs the **apt** package manager if it is not already present.

Using 'apt' to Manage Packages

We shall explore how to use **apt** for various package management tasks in our AlphaProject environment.

Updating the Package List

Before installing or updating packages, it is essential to refresh the package list to ensure you're accessing the latest versions:

```
$ sudo apt update
```

This command fetches the latest package information from all configured repositories.

Upgrading Packages

To upgrade all installed packages to their latest versions, use:

```
$ sudo apt upgrade
```

For a more comprehensive upgrade that also removes obsolete packages, use:

```
$ sudo apt full-upgrade
```

Installing Packages

To install a new package, use the **apt install** command followed by the package name. For example, to install Git:

```
$ sudo apt install git
```

apt will handle downloading and installing Git along with any necessary dependencies.

Removing Packages

To remove a package that is no longer needed, use the **apt remove** command:

```
$ sudo apt remove git
```

If you want to remove a package along with its configuration files, use:

```
$ sudo apt purge git
```

To clean up unnecessary dependencies, use:

```
$ sudo apt autoremove
```

Searching for Packages

If you're unsure about the exact name of a package, you can search for it using **apt search**:

```
$ apt search git
```

This command lists all packages related to the keyword **git**.

Viewing Package Information

To view detailed information about a specific package, use **apt show** followed by the package name:

```
$ apt show git
```

This command provides details about the package, including its description, version, dependencies, and more.

Holding and Unholding Packages

To prevent a package from being updated, you can hold it using:

```
$ sudo apt-mark hold git
```

To allow the package to be updated again, use:

```
$ sudo apt-mark unhold git
```

Adding and Removing Repositories

Repositories are sources where **apt** fetches packages. Sometimes, you may need to add third-party repositories to access specific software.

To add a new repository, use **add-apt-repository**. For example, to add a PPA (Personal Package Archive) for the latest Node.js:

```
$ sudo add-apt-repository ppa:chris-lea/node.js

$ sudo apt update
```

This command adds the repository and updates the package list to include the new software.

To remove a repository, you need to edit the sources list:

```
$ sudo nano /etc/apt/sources.list
```

Find the repository you want to remove and delete the corresponding line.

Sample Workflow: Managing Packages for AlphaProject

Installing a Web Server and Database

- Install Apache Web Server:

```
$ sudo apt install apache2
```

- Verify the installation:

```
$ systemctl status apache2
```

- Install MySQL Database Server:

```
$ sudo apt install mysql-server
```

- Secure the MySQL installation:

```
$ sudo mysql_secure_installation
```

- Install PHP:

```
$ sudo apt install php libapache2-mod-php php-mysql
```

- Verify PHP Installation:

Create a test PHP file:

```
$ sudo nano /var/www/html/info.php
```

Add the following line:

```
<?php phpinfo(); ?>
```

Access **http://your_server_ip/info.php** in a web browser to verify PHP.

Setting up a Development Environment

- Install Git:

```
$ sudo apt install git
```

- Install Node.js and npm:

```
$ sudo apt install nodejs npm
```

- Install Docker:

```
$ sudo apt install docker.io
```

- Start and enable Docker:

```
$ sudo systemctl start docker

$ sudo systemctl enable docker
```

- Install Visual Studio Code:

Add the Microsoft repository:

```
$ sudo apt update

$ sudo apt install software-properties-common apt-
transport-https wget

$ wget -q
https://packages.microsoft.com/keys/microsoft.asc -O- |
sudo apt-key add -

$ sudo add-apt-repository "deb [arch=amd64]
https://packages.microsoft.com/repos/vscode stable main"
```

- Install Visual Studio Code:

```
$ sudo apt install code
```

Using this procedure, you can be confident that your web server, database server, development environment, and containerization platform are all up and running smoothly with the help of **apt**. A well-versed user of **apt** can efficiently manage software packages, keeping their Linux system secure, up-to-date, and AlphaProject-ready.

Managing Dependencies

When dealing with several libraries, packages, and shared files in Linux, dependency management becomes quite important for keeping everything running smoothly. To ensure proper operation, software often requires supplementary packages or libraries, which are known as dependencies. To avoid conflicts and mistakes, it is important to use effective dependency management to make sure all the necessary components are present and up-to-date.

Finding Dependencies

To manage dependencies, you first need to identify what dependencies a package has. This can be done using **apt** commands on Debian-based systems.

Finding Dependencies with 'apt'

To list the dependencies of a package, use the **apt-cache depends** command:

```
$ apt-cache depends git
```

This command shows all the packages that **git** depends on.

Finding Reverse Dependencies

To see what packages depend on a specific package (reverse dependencies), use:

```
$ apt-cache rdepends git
```

This command lists all the packages that depend on **git**.

Updating Dependencies

Keeping dependencies up-to-date is essential for security and functionality. To update all packages, including their dependencies, use the **apt upgrade** command.

```
$ sudo apt update

$ sudo apt upgrade
```

This ensures that all installed packages and their dependencies are updated to the latest versions.

Modifying Dependencies

Sometimes, you may need to manually modify or configure dependencies. This could involve installing specific versions of a package, changing configuration files, or setting environment variables.

Installing Specific Versions

To install a specific version of a package, use the **apt install** command with the version number:

```
$ sudo apt install package=version
```

For example:

```
$ sudo apt install nginx=1.18.0-0ubuntu1
```

This installs the specified version of **nginx**.

Editing Configuration Files

Configuration files for dependencies are usually located in the **/etc** directory. For example, to edit the configuration file for **nginx**:

```
$ sudo nano /etc/nginx/nginx.conf
```

Make the necessary changes and save the file.

Setting Environment Variables

Sometimes dependencies require specific environment variables. To set an environment variable, use the **export** command:

```
$ export VARIABLE_NAME=value
```

For example:

```
$ export JAVA_HOME=/usr/lib/jvm/java-11-openjdk-amd64
```

Add this line to **~/.bashrc** or **/etc/environment** to make it persistent across sessions.

Fixing Dependency Issues

Dependency issues can occur due to missing, broken, or conflicting packages. **apt** provides tools to diagnose and fix these issues.

Fixing Broken Packages

To fix broken dependencies, use the **--fix-broken** option:

```
$ sudo apt --fix-broken install
```

This command attempts to correct any broken dependencies on your system.

Resolving Conflicts

If there are conflicts between packages, you might need to remove or forcefully install specific packages. Use the **dpkg** command to forcefully remove a problematic package:

```
$ sudo dpkg --remove --force-remove-reinstreq package-
name
```

Then, use **apt** to install the correct package:

```
$ sudo apt install package-name
```

Checking for Missing Dependencies

To check for missing dependencies, use the **check** command:

```
$ sudo apt check
```

This command checks the package database for consistency and reports any issues.

Changing Permissions of Users/Applications for Libraries and Shared Files

Managing permissions ensures that users and applications have the appropriate access to libraries and shared files.

Changing File Permissions

Use the **chmod** command to change file permissions. For example, to give read and write permissions to the owner and group for a file:

```
$ sudo chmod 660 /path/to/file
```

Changing Ownership

Use the **chown** command to change the ownership of files and directories. For example, to change the owner to **user** and the group to **group**:

```
$ sudo chown user:group /path/to/file
```

Setting Permissions for Libraries

Libraries are typically stored in **/usr/lib** or **/usr/local/lib**. Ensure that the necessary permissions are set so that applications can access these libraries. For example:

```
$ sudo chmod 755 /usr/lib/libexample.so

$ sudo chown root:root /usr/lib/libexample.so
```

Managing User Permissions

To manage user permissions for accessing applications and files, use the **usermod** command to modify user groups and permissions. For example, to add a user to the **sudo** group:

```
$ sudo usermod -aG sudo username
```

Sample Program: Managing Dependencies for AlphaProject

We shall apply these concepts to manage dependencies for a web server stack in AlphaProject.

Installing Apache, MySQL, and PHP (LAMP Stack)

Install Apache:

```
$ sudo apt install apache2
```

Check dependencies:

```
$ apt-cache depends apache2
```

Install MySQL:

```
$ sudo apt install mysql-server
```

Secure MySQL:

```
$ sudo mysql_secure_installation
```

Install PHP:

```
$ sudo apt install php libapache2-mod-php php-mysql
```

Check for Missing Dependencies:

```
$ sudo apt check
```

Fix Broken Packages:

```
$ sudo apt --fix-broken install
```

Modifying Configuration Files

Apache Configuration:

```
$ sudo nano /etc/apache2/apache2.conf
```

MySQL Configuration:

```
$ sudo nano /etc/mysql/my.cnf
```

PHP Configuration:

```
$ sudo nano /etc/php/7.4/apache2/php.ini
```

Setting Environment Variables

Set PHP Home:

```
$ export PHP_HOME=/usr/lib/php
```

Changing Permissions

Apache Web Directory:

```
$ sudo chmod -R 755 /var/www/html

$ sudo chown -R www-data:www-data /var/www/html
```

MySQL Data Directory:

```
$ sudo chmod -R 700 /var/lib/mysql

$ sudo chown -R mysql:mysql /var/lib/mysql
```

Make sure all the components you need are there, set appropriately, and securely accessible in your Linux system by mastering and implementing these dependency management approaches. Especially for complicated projects like AlphaProject, this method keeps the system running smoothly and efficiently.

Configuring System Hardware

One of the most important aspects of system administration is the configuration of system hardware, which enables you to optimize and personalize the resources that are available to your projects. Right now, we're going to learn about setting up WiFi networks, firewalls, and other external devices to function with AlphaProject.

Configuring WiFi Networks

To manage WiFi networks on your Linux system, you can use tools like **nmcli** (NetworkManager Command Line Interface) and **wpa_supplicant**.

Using 'nmcli'

- Listing Available WiFi Networks:

```
$ nmcli device wifi list
```

This command lists all available WiFi networks.

- Connecting to a WiFi Network:

```
$ nmcli device wifi connect 'SSID' password
'your_password'
```

Replace **SSID** with the name of the WiFi network and **your_password** with the network password.

- Checking Connection Status:

```
$ nmcli device status
```

This command shows the status of network devices.

Using 'wpa_supplicant'

- Create a WPA Configuration File:

```
$ sudo nano /etc/wpa_supplicant/wpa_supplicant.conf
```

- Add the following configuration:

```
network={
 ssid="SSID"
 psk="your_password"
}
```

Replace **SSID** with your network's SSID and **your_password** with the network password.

- Start **wpa_supplicant**:

```
$ sudo wpa_supplicant -B -i wlan0 -c
/etc/wpa_supplicant/wpa_supplicant.conf
```

This command runs **wpa_supplicant** in the background, connecting to the specified WiFi network.

- Obtain an IP Address:

```
$ sudo dhclient wlan0
```

This command uses DHCP to obtain an IP address for the **wlan0** interface.

Configuring Firewalls

Firewalls are crucial for securing your system by controlling incoming and outgoing network traffic. **ufw** (Uncomplicated Firewall) is a user-friendly interface for managing iptables firewall rules.

Using 'ufw'

- Enable **ufw**:

```
$ sudo ufw enable
```

- Allowing SSH Connections:

```
$ sudo ufw allow ssh
```

This command ensures that SSH connections are permitted.

- Allowing HTTP and HTTPS Traffic:

```
$ sudo ufw allow http

$ sudo ufw allow https
```

- Denying Specific Traffic:

To block specific traffic, use the **deny** command. For example, to deny all incoming traffic on port 8080:

```
$ sudo ufw deny 8080
```

- Viewing Firewall Status and Rules:

```
$ sudo ufw status verbose
```

Using iptables

For more advanced firewall configurations, you can use **iptables**.

- Allowing SSH Connections:

```
$ sudo iptables -A INPUT -p tcp --dport 22 -j ACCEPT
```

- Allowing HTTP and HTTPS Traffic:

```
$ sudo iptables -A INPUT -p tcp --dport 80 -j ACCEPT
$ sudo iptables -A INPUT -p tcp --dport 443 -j ACCEPT
```

- Blocking a Specific IP Address:

```
$ sudo iptables -A INPUT -s 192.168.1.100 -j DROP
```

This command blocks all traffic from IP address **192.168.1.100**.

- Saving iptables Rules:

After configuring iptables rules, save them to ensure they persist across reboots:

```
$ sudo sh -c "iptables-save > /etc/iptables/rules.v4"
```

Configuring External Devices

External devices, such as USB drives, printers, and other peripherals, often require specific configurations to function correctly.

Mounting USB Drives

- List Available Devices:

```
$ lsblk
```

This command lists all block devices, including USB drives.

- Create a Mount Point:

```
$ sudo mkdir /mnt/usb
```

- Mount the USB Drive:

```
$ sudo mount /dev/sdX1 /mnt/usb
```

Replace **sdX1** with the appropriate device identifier from **lsblk**.

- Access the USB Drive:

You can now access the contents of the USB drive at **/mnt/usb**.

- Unmount the USB Drive:

```
$ sudo umount /mnt/usb
```

Configuring Printers

- Install CUPS (Common Unix Printing System):

```
$ sudo apt install cups
```

- Start and Enable CUPS:

```
$ sudo systemctl start cups

$ sudo systemctl enable cups
```

- Add Your User to the **lpadmin** Group:

```
$ sudo usermod -aG lpadmin your_username
```

- Access the CUPS Web Interface:

Open a web browser and navigate to **http://localhost:631**. Use the web interface to add and configure printers.

Connecting to Bluetooth Devices

- Install Bluetooth Utilities:

```
$ sudo apt install bluetooth bluez blueman
```

- Start and Enable Bluetooth Service:

```
$ sudo systemctl start bluetooth
```

```
$ sudo systemctl enable bluetooth
```

- Scan for Bluetooth Devices:

```
$ bluetoothctl
```

Within the **bluetoothctl** shell, use:

```
[bluetooth]# scan on
```

- Pair and Connect to a Device:

```
[bluetooth]# pair MAC_address

[bluetooth]# connect MAC_address
```

Sample Program: Configuring System Hardware for AlphaProject

Configuring Network Settings

- Connect to a WiFi Network:

```
$ nmcli device wifi connect 'AlphaWiFi' password
'alpha_password'
```

Setting up the Firewall

- Enable Firewall and Allow Essential Services:

```
$ sudo ufw enable

$ sudo ufw allow ssh

$ sudo ufw allow http

$ sudo ufw allow https
```

Mounting and Using an External USB Drive

- Identify and Mount the USB Drive:

```
$ lsblk

$ sudo mkdir /mnt/usb

$ sudo mount /dev/sdb1 /mnt/usb
```

- Access and Use the USB Drive:

```
$ cp /mnt/usb/project_files/* /projects/AlphaProject/
```

Configuring a Printer

- Install and Setup CUPS:

```
$ sudo apt install cups

$ sudo systemctl start cups

$ sudo systemctl enable cups
```

- Add User to **lpadmin** Group and Access CUPS:

```
$ sudo usermod -aG lpadmin alphauser

$ sudo service cups restart
```

- Configure Printer via Web Interface:

Open **http://localhost:631** and follow the instructions to add the printer.

If you take the time to learn and use these settings, you'll be able to set up AlphaProject with a solid foundation and plenty of room to grow. This involves controlling external devices to increase efficiency and resource use, installing firewalls for security, and setting up WiFi networks.

Upgrading Kernel

Part of what makes Linux an OS is its kernel, which connects programs to the hardware. It keeps everything running smoothly, coordinates the flow of data between programs and hardware, and monitors resource usage. The kernel is in charge of managing processes, memory, device drivers, and system calls.

Role of Kernel in System Functioning

The kernel plays several critical roles:

1. Manages the execution of processes, including multitasking, scheduling, and resource allocation.
2. Handles memory allocation for processes, manages the virtual memory, and ensures efficient use of RAM.
3. Provides a standardized interface for hardware devices, managing device drivers and ensuring proper communication between hardware and software.
4. Manages data storage, file operations, and access to different file systems.
5. Enforces security policies, manages user permissions, and ensures system integrity.

Vulnerabilities to the Kernel

Due to its critical role, the kernel is a prime target for vulnerabilities that can compromise system security and stability:

1. Exploiting kernel vulnerabilities to gain unauthorized access or higher privileges.
2. Exploiting kernel bugs to crash the system or render services unavailable.
3. Leaking sensitive information from the kernel memory.
4. Injecting malicious code to be executed with kernel-level privileges.

Upgrading the Kernel

Keeping the kernel up-to-date is crucial for maintaining security, performance, and compatibility with new hardware and software. Let us upgrade the kernel in our Linux environment for AlphaProject.

Checking the Current Kernel Version

First, check the current kernel version:

```
$ uname -r
```

This command outputs the version of the running kernel, for example, **`5.4.0-42-generic`**.

Upgrading the Kernel on Debian-based Systems (Ubuntu)

- Update Package Lists:

```
$ sudo apt update
```

- Install the **`linux-image-generic`** Package:

The **`linux-image-generic`** package installs the latest stable kernel available in the repositories.

```
$ sudo apt install linux-image-generic
```

- Reboot the System:

After installation, reboot the system to boot into the new kernel.

```
$ sudo reboot
```

- Verify the New Kernel Version:

After rebooting, check the kernel version again to ensure the update was successful:

```
$ uname -r
```

Upgrading to a Specific Kernel Version

Sometimes, you might need to upgrade to a specific kernel version not available in the standard repositories. For this, you can download and install the kernel manually.

- Download the Kernel Packages:

Visit the Ubuntu Kernel PPA and download the desired kernel version. For example:

```
$ wget https://kernel.ubuntu.com/~kernel-
ppa/mainline/v5.11.10/amd64/linux-headers-5.11.10-
051110_5.11.10-051110.202103200734_all.deb

$ wget https://kernel.ubuntu.com/~kernel-
ppa/mainline/v5.11.10/amd64/linux-headers-5.11.10-051110-
generic_5.11.10-051110.202103200734_amd64.deb
```

```
$ wget https://kernel.ubuntu.com/~kernel-
ppa/mainline/v5.11.10/amd64/linux-image-unsigned-5.11.10-
051110-generic_5.11.10-051110.202103200734_amd64.deb

$ wget https://kernel.ubuntu.com/~kernel-
ppa/mainline/v5.11.10/amd64/linux-modules-5.11.10-051110-
generic_5.11.10-051110.202103200734_amd64.deb
```

- Install the Kernel Packages:

```
$ sudo dpkg -i *.deb
```

- Update GRUB Configuration:

After installing the new kernel, update the GRUB bootloader configuration.

```
$ sudo update-grub
```

Reboot the System:

```
$ sudo reboot
```

Verify the New Kernel Version:

```
$ uname -r
```

Upgrading the Kernel on Red Hat-based Systems (CentOS, Fedora)

- Update Package Lists:

```
$ sudo yum update
```

- Install the **kernel** Package:

The **kernel** package installs the latest stable kernel available in the repositories.

```
$ sudo yum install kernel
```

- Reboot the System:

```
$ sudo reboot
```

- Verify the New Kernel Version:

```
$ uname -r
```

Handling Kernel Modules

Kernel modules are pieces of code that can be loaded and unloaded into the kernel upon demand. They extend the functionality of the kernel without the need to reboot the system.

- Listing Loaded Modules:

To list all loaded kernel modules, use:

```
$ lsmod
```

- Loading a Kernel Module:

To load a kernel module, use the **modprobe** command:

```
$ sudo modprobe module_name
```

- Unloading a Kernel Module:

To unload a kernel module, use the **modprobe -r** command:

```
$ sudo modprobe -r module_name
```

- Checking Module Information:

To check information about a specific module, use:

```
$ modinfo module_name
```

Managing Kernel Updates with UKUU

For Ubuntu and other Debian-based systems, the **UKUU** (Ubuntu Kernel Update Utility) tool simplifies kernel updates.

- Install UKUU:

```
$ sudo add-apt-repository ppa:teejee2008/ppa

$ sudo apt update

$ sudo apt install ukuu
```

- Launch UKUU:

```
$ sudo ukuu-gtk
```

This command opens a graphical interface where you can select and install different kernel versions.

To automate kernel updates and ensure you always have the latest security patches and features, you can set up a cron job or use a system automation tool like **cron-apt**.

- Install cron-apt:

```
$ sudo apt install cron-apt
```

- Configure cron-apt:

Edit the configuration file:

```
$ sudo nano /etc/cron-apt/config
```

Set it to automatically download and install updates:

```
APTCOMMAND=/usr/bin/apt-get

OPTIONS="-o quiet=1"

MAILON="always"
```

If you know what the kernel is and how to keep it updated, you can keep your Linux system secure, stable, and up-to-date with all the newest software and hardware improvements.

Handling Device Drivers

An operating system and its hardware components can't communicate without device drivers. System stability and performance are greatly affected by out-of-date device drivers. In this section, we will look at the process of finding, updating, and automating the process of updating device drivers in a Linux system.

Finding All Available Drivers

To list all available drivers on your system, you can use several tools and commands.

Using 'lsmod'

The **lsmod** command lists all currently loaded kernel modules (drivers):

```
$ lsmod
```

This command outputs a list of all loaded modules, including their names, sizes, and usage counts.

Using 'lspci'

The **lspci** command lists all PCI devices and their associated drivers:

```
$ lspci -k
```

This command provides detailed information about PCI devices and their corresponding kernel drivers.

Using 'lshw'

The **lshw** (list hardware) command displays detailed information about hardware components, including drivers:

```
$ sudo lshw -c network
```

Replace **network** with the desired hardware class (e.g., **network**, **storage**, **display**) to get specific information.

Finding Drivers with Available Updates

To find out if there are updates available for your drivers, you can use package management tools and additional utilities.

Using 'apt'

- Update Package Lists:

```
$ sudo apt update
```

- List Upgradable Packages:

```
$ apt list --upgradable
```

This command lists all packages with available updates, including drivers.

Using 'ubuntu-drivers'

The **ubuntu-drivers** tool is specifically designed for handling proprietary drivers:

```
$ ubuntu-drivers list
```

This command lists all available drivers that can be installed or updated.

Using 'fwupdmgr'

The **fwupdmgr** (Firmware Update Manager) tool can be used to check for firmware updates:

```
$ sudo fwupdmgr get-updates
```

This command checks for available firmware updates for your system.

Updating Drivers

Once you've identified which drivers need updates, you can proceed to update them.

Updating Drivers with 'apt'

- Update Specific Packages:

```
$ sudo apt install --only-upgrade package_name
```

Replace **package_name** with the name of the package you want to update.

- Update All Packages:

```
$ sudo apt upgrade
```

This command updates all installed packages to their latest versions.

Updating Proprietary Drivers with 'ubuntu-drivers'

Install Recommended Drivers:

```
$ sudo ubuntu-drivers autoinstall
```

This command installs all recommended proprietary drivers.

Updating Firmware with 'fwupdmgr'

Apply Firmware Updates:

```
$ sudo fwupdmgr update
```

This command downloads and installs available firmware updates.

Automating Driver Updates

Automating the process of updating drivers ensures that your system remains up-to-date with minimal manual intervention.

Using 'cron-apt' for Regular Updates

- Install **cron-apt**:

```
$ sudo apt install cron-apt
```

- Configure **cron-apt**:

Edit the configuration file:

```
$ sudo nano /etc/cron-apt/config
```

Set it to automatically download and install updates:

```
APTCOMMAND=/usr/bin/apt-get
```

```
OPTIONS="-o quiet=1"

MAILON="always"
```

- Add a Specific Command for Driver Updates:

Create or edit the configuration file in **/etc/cron-apt/action.d/** to include driver updates:

```
$ sudo nano /etc/cron-apt/action.d/3-driver-updates
```

- Add the following lines:

```
upgrade --with-new-pkgs -y
```

Using 'fwupdmgr' in a Cron Job

Edit the crontab for the root user:

```
$ sudo crontab -e
```

Add the following line to check for firmware updates daily:

```
0 3 * * * /usr/bin/fwupdmgr get-updates &&
/usr/bin/fwupdmgr update
```

Sample Program: Updating and Automating Driver Updates

Finding Current Drivers

- List Loaded Kernel Modules:

```
$ lsmod
```

- List PCI Devices and Drivers:

```
$ lspci -k
```

Identifying Available Driver Updates

- Update Package Lists:

```
$ sudo apt update
```

- List Upgradable Packages:

```
$ apt list --upgradable
```

- Check for Firmware Updates:

```
$ sudo fwupdmgr get-updates
```

Updating Drivers

- Update All Packages:

```
$ sudo apt upgrade
```

- Install Recommended Proprietary Drivers:

```
$ sudo ubuntu-drivers autoinstall
```

- Apply Firmware Updates:

```
$ sudo fwupdmgr update
```

Automating Updates

- Setup **cron-apt**:

```
$ sudo apt install cron-apt
$ sudo nano /etc/cron-apt/config
```

- Add to the configuration file:

```
APTCOMMAND=/usr/bin/apt-get

OPTIONS="-o quiet=1"

MAILON="always"
```

- Create a Driver Update Action File:

```
$ sudo nano /etc/cron-apt/action.d/3-driver-updates
```

- Add the following lines:

```
upgrade --with-new-pkgs -y
```

- Schedule Firmware Updates:

```
$ sudo crontab -e
```

- Add to crontab:

```
0 3 * * * /usr/bin/fwupdmgr get-updates &&
/usr/bin/fwupdmgr update
```

Following these instructions will help you manage and update your AlphaProject device drivers efficiently. This will ensure that your system is always up-to-date and secure.

Setting up and Managing Repositories

Linux systems cannot function without repositories, that contain software packages. When you set up and manage repositories correctly, your system will always have access to the most recent versions of the programs you need for your projects. In this part, we will go over the basics of using command-line tools to create, manage, and secure Linux repositories.

Setting up Repositories

To set up repositories, you can add entries to your package manager's source list. On Debian-based systems like Ubuntu, this involves editing files in **/etc/apt/sources.list** or adding new files in **/etc/apt/sources.list.d/**.

Adding a Repository

Add a Repository Using **add-apt-repository**:

```
$ sudo add-apt-repository ppa:repository_name
```

This command adds a PPA (Personal Package Archive) to your system. Replace **repository_name** with the actual PPA name.

Manually Adding a Repository

Edit the sources list file:

```
$ sudo nano /etc/apt/sources.list
```

Add a new line with the repository details:

```
deb http://archive.ubuntu.com/ubuntu/ bionic main
universe
```

Replace **http://archive.ubuntu.com/ubuntu/** with the URL of your desired repository and **bionic** with your distribution codename.

Add a Repository Key

Some repositories require you to add a GPG key to verify package authenticity. Use the following command to add a key:

```
$ wget -qO - https://gitforgits.com/key.gpg | sudo apt-
key add -
```

Replace **https://gitforgits.com/key.gpg** with the URL to the key file.

Update Package List

After adding the repository, update the package list:

```
$ sudo apt update
```

Managing Repositories

Managing repositories involves enabling, disabling, removing, and prioritizing them.

Enabling/Disabling Repositories

Repositories can be enabled or disabled by commenting or uncommenting lines in the source list files.

- Disable a Repository:

```
$ sudo nano /etc/apt/sources.list
```

Comment out the repository line by adding a **#** at the beginning:

```
# deb http://archive.ubuntu.com/ubuntu/ bionic main
universe
```

- Enable a Repository:

Uncomment the repository line by removing the **#**:

```
deb http://archive.ubuntu.com/ubuntu/ bionic main
universe
```

Removing a Repository

To remove a repository, delete its entry from the source list file.

```
$ sudo nano /etc/apt/sources.list
```

Delete the corresponding repository line:

```
deb http://archive.ubuntu.com/ubuntu/ bionic main
universe
```

Using 'apt' Preferences

You can control the priority of repositories using the **`/etc/apt/preferences`** file.

- Create or Edit the Preferences File:

```
$ sudo nano /etc/apt/preferences
```

- Add entries to set priority:

```
Package: *

Pin: release a=bionic

Pin-Priority: 500


Package: *

Pin: release o=Ubuntu

Pin-Priority: 700
```

Protecting Repositories

Repository protection ensures that the packages you download and install are authentic and have not been tampered with.

GPC Keys

GPG keys are used to sign repositories and verify the integrity of packages.

- Add a GPG Key:

```
$ wget -qO - https://gitforgits.com/key.gpg | sudo apt-
key add -
```

- List Installed GPG Keys:

```
$ apt-key list
```

- Remove a GPG Key:

```
$ sudo apt-key del key_id
```

Enabling Secure APT

Secure APT ensures that packages are downloaded and verified using GPG signatures.

- Check Secure APT Configuration:

Edit the configuration file:

```
$ sudo nano /etc/apt/apt.conf.d/10secure
```

Ensure it contains the following:

```
APT::Get::AllowUnauthenticated "false";
```

- Using **`apt-secure`**:

`apt-secure` is integrated with **`apt`** to ensure package authenticity.

During the update process, **`apt`** will automatically verify package signatures. If there are issues with verification, you will receive a warning.

Sample Program: Setting up and Managing Repositories for AlphaProject

Adding a Repository

- Add a PPA for AlphaProject:

```
$ sudo add-apt-repository ppa:alpha/ppa
```

- Add Repository Key:

```
$ wget -qO - https://alpha.com/key.gpg | sudo apt-key add
-
```

- Update Package List:

```
$ sudo apt update
```

Managing Repositories

- Enable a Repository:

```
$ sudo nano /etc/apt/sources.list
```

- Uncomment the line:

```
deb http://archive.ubuntu.com/ubuntu/ focal main universe
```

- Disable a Repository:

```
$ sudo nano /etc/apt/sources.list
```

- Comment the line:

```
# deb http://archive.ubuntu.com/ubuntu/ focal main
universe
```

- Remove a Repository:

```
$ sudo nano /etc/apt/sources.list
```

- Delete the line:

```
deb http://archive.ubuntu.com/ubuntu/ focal main universe
```

Setting Priorities with 'apt' Preferences

- Edit Preferences File:

```
$ sudo nano /etc/apt/preferences
```

- Add priority settings:

```
Package: *

Pin: release a=focal

Pin-Priority: 600
```

```
Package: *

Pin: release o=Ubuntu

Pin-Priority: 800
```

Protecting Repositories

- Check Installed GPG Keys:

```
$ apt-key list
```

- Add a GPG Key:

```
$ wget -qO - https://alpha.com/key.gpg | sudo apt-key add
-
```

- Enable Secure APT:

```
$ sudo nano /etc/apt/apt.conf.d/10secure
```

- Ensure the file contains:

```
APT::Get::AllowUnauthenticated "false";
```

This method offers a safe and dependable way to handle software installation and update management. By adhering to these guidelines, you will be able to successfully establish and administer AlphaProject repositories, giving you access to all required software packages without compromising our system's security or integrity.

Installing and Configuring Virtual Machines with VirtualBox

To create, test, and release software in sandboxed settings, virtual machines (VMs) are necessary. They simplify the management of various development environments, test settings, and legacy programs by enabling the running of numerous operating systems on the same physical machine. VirtualBox supports the creation and management of virtual machines across various operating systems, including Linux, Windows, and macOS. By offering uniform and reproducible environments, virtual machines help streamline development and testing procedures for AlphaProject.

Installing VirtualBox

To install VirtualBox on a Debian-based system like Ubuntu, follow these steps:

- Update Your System:

```
$ sudo apt update
```

- Install Required Dependencies:

```
$ sudo apt install -y wget gnupg2
```

- Download and add the VirtualBox signing key:

```
$ wget -q
https://www.virtualbox.org/download/oracle_vbox_2016.asc
-O- | sudo apt-key add -

$ wget -q
https://www.virtualbox.org/download/oracle_vbox.asc -O- |
sudo apt-key add -
```

- Add the VirtualBox repository to your sources list:

```
$ sudo add-apt-repository "deb [arch=amd64]
http://download.virtualbox.org/virtualbox/debian
$(lsb_release -cs) contrib"
```

- Install VirtualBox:

```
$ sudo apt update
```

```
$ sudo apt install -y virtualbox-6.1
```

- Check the version of VirtualBox to ensure it is installed correctly:

```
$ vboxmanage --version
```

Setting up a Virtual Machine for AlphaProject

Once VirtualBox is installed, you can create and configure a virtual machine for AlphaProject.

- Open VirtualBox from the application menu or by running:

```
$ virtualbox
```

- Create a New Virtual Machine:
  - Click on the "New" button to create a new VM.
  - Enter the name of the VM (e.g., "AlphaProjectVM"), select the type (Linux), and version (Ubuntu 64-bit).
  - Click "Next" to proceed.
- Allocate Memory:
  - Allocate memory (RAM) for the VM. For development purposes, at least 2GB (2048MB) is recommended.
  - Click "Next" to proceed.
- Create a Virtual Hard Disk:
  - Select "Create a virtual hard disk now" and click "Create".
  - Choose the hard disk file type. The default VDI (VirtualBox Disk Image) is suitable.
  - Choose "Dynamically allocated" to allow the disk to grow as needed.
  - Specify the size of the virtual hard disk. For development, at least 20GB is recommended.
  - Click "Create" to finish creating the virtual hard disk.
- Configure the Virtual Machine:
  - Select the newly created VM and click on "Settings".

    - In the "System" tab, ensure the allocated RAM is appropriate and that "Enable EFI" is unchecked unless you need UEFI.
    - In the "Processor" tab, allocate at least 2 CPU cores if available.
    - In the "Display" tab, increase the Video Memory to 128MB for better graphical performance.
- Attach an ISO Image:
    - In the "Storage" tab, click on the "Empty" CD icon under "Controller: IDE".
    - Click on the CD icon next to "Optical Drive" and select "Choose a disk file".
    - Select the ISO image of the Ubuntu installation media you downloaded earlier.
    - Click "OK" to save the settings.
- Start the Virtual Machine:
    - Select the VM and click "Start".
    - The VM will boot from the ISO image, starting the Ubuntu installation process.

Installing Ubuntu on the Virtual Machine

Follow these steps to install Ubuntu on your new VM:

- Boot from ISO:
    - The VM should boot from the attached ISO. Select "Install Ubuntu" from the boot menu.
- Choose Language and Keyboard Layout:
    - Follow the prompts to select your preferred language and keyboard layout.
- Update and Other Software:
    - Select "Normal installation" and check "Download updates while installing Ubuntu" for a smoother installation process.
    - Click "Continue".
- Disk Partitioning:
    - Choose "Erase disk and install Ubuntu" as this VM will be used for development and testing purposes.
    - Click "Install Now" and confirm any prompts to write changes to the disk.
- Setup User Account:

    - Enter your name, the name of your computer (e.g., AlphaProjectVM), and choose a username and password.
    - Click "Continue" to proceed with the installation.
- Complete Installation:
    - The installer will copy files and configure the system. This may take some time.
    - Once the installation is complete, click "Restart Now" to reboot the VM.
- Remove the Installation Media:
    - When prompted, remove the installation media by clicking "Devices" in the VirtualBox menu, selecting "Optical Drives", and unchecking the ISO file.
    - Press "Enter" to reboot.

Post-Installation Configuration

After installing Ubuntu on the VM, perform some basic configurations to prepare the VM for development.

- Update the System:
    - Open a terminal and update the package list and upgrade installed packages:

```
$ sudo apt update

$ sudo apt upgrade -y
```

- Install Essential Packages:
    - Install development tools and libraries needed for AlphaProject:

```
$ sudo apt install -y build-essential git curl vim
```

- Install VirtualBox Guest Additions:
    - Guest Additions provide better integration between the host and guest systems, including shared folders and improved graphics performance.
    - In the VirtualBox menu, click "Devices" and select "Insert Guest Additions CD image".
    - If prompted to download the ISO, allow it to do so.
    - Mount the CD image and install the Guest Additions:

```
$ sudo mount /dev/cdrom /mnt

$ sudo /mnt/VBoxLinuxAdditions.run
```

- Reboot the VM:

```
$ sudo reboot
```

- Setup Shared Folders:
  - To enable shared folders between the host and the VM, go to the VM settings in VirtualBox, click on "Shared Folders", and add a new shared folder.
  - Make sure to check "Auto-mount" and "Make Permanent".
  - Access the shared folder from the VM:

```
$ sudo usermod -aG vboxsf your_username
```

- Networking Configuration:
  - Ensure the VM is connected to the network. The default NAT networking mode should suffice for most purposes.
  - To use a bridged network, go to the VM settings, click on "Network", and select "Bridged Adapter".
- Install Specific Software for AlphaProject:
  - Install any additional software or dependencies specific to AlphaProject. For instance, if your project requires Node.js:

```
$ curl -sL https://deb.nodesource.com/setup_14.x | sudo -
E bash -

$ sudo apt install -y nodejs
```

The ability to handle many development environments, test setups, and maintain consistency across the project's stages is made possible by this above structured steps.

Summary

The primary emphasis of this chapter was the process of configuring, deploying, and upgrading hardware and software for Linux systems. At the outset of the chapter, we learned how to use apt and yum, two of the most important tools for managing software packages on Debian-and Red Hat-based systems, respectively. To make sure all the required parts were available and working properly, we looked at the process of managing dependencies, which included finding, updating, and modifying them. For effective package management, this required the use of tools such as apt-cache dependencies and apt-get.

Managing external devices like USB drives and printers, establishing firewalls with ufw and iptables, and setting up WiFi networks with nmcli and wpa_supplicant were all addressed in the chapter on configuring system hardware. We covered why it is important to update the kernel for better security and speed, and we went over the specifics of how to do it on Debian and Red Hat systems. Another important subject was managing device drivers, wherein techniques for locating, updating, and automating driver updates were showcased utilizing utilities such as fwupdmgr, ubuntu-drivers, lsmod, and lspci.

In order to guarantee access to the most recent software packages, the process of setting up and managing repositories was thoroughly explained, including how to add, remove, and prioritize repositories. Enabling secure APT to preserve package integrity and protecting repositories using GPG keys were also covered in the chapter.

At last, the chapter delves into the process of setting up VirtualBox and creating virtual machines. It went over everything you need to know about virtual machines (VMs) for testing and development, including how to install VirtualBox and set up a VM for AlphaProject. We also covered post-installation adjustments to enhance the development environment of the virtual machine, including installing necessary programs, VirtualBox Guest Additions, and shared folders. Thanks to your detailed introduction, I now know how to manage Linux systems' software and hardware.

CHAPTER IV: USER AND PERMISSION MANAGEMENT

Overview

In this final chapter, we will look at user and permission management, which is critical for maintaining system security and ensuring that users have proper access levels. In the first section of the final chapter, you will get the necessary information to easily create, edit, and delete user accounts. To make sure users have the right permissions and environment settings for their responsibilities, we'll also go over how to manage and personalize user profiles.

Next, you will learn how to use Linux's permission model to manage who may access what files and folders by going over the basics of file ownership and permissions. You will also gain knowledge of Access Control Lists (ACLs), a way to specify permissions at a finer level than the typical user-group-other paradigm. Another crucial part is managing user sessions, where you'll learn about commands and tools to keep tabs on and manage all of the sessions that are currently running on your system.

We will also learn how to set up sudo for administrative tasks so that specific users can safely execute privileged actions. The chapter will go over password rules and how to manage them so that you may have strong authentication procedures. Additionally, you will gain knowledge about PAMs, which provide a versatile way to include different authentication methods. At last, we'll go over how to manage group memberships to make users more organized and streamline permission management. This way, we can make sure that only appropriate individuals have access to the resources they need. The goal of this chapter is to provide you the tools you need to become an expert Linux user and permission manager.

Creating and Managing User Accounts

Creating User Accounts

Creating and managing user accounts is a fundamental task in Linux administration, essential for controlling access to system resources. To create user accounts, you use the **useradd** command, followed by various options to specify user details.

There are three primary types of user accounts: regular users, system users, and service users.

Creating Regular User Accounts

Regular users are typical users who log in and use the system.

- Create a Regular User:

```
$ sudo useradd -m -s /bin/bash username
```

This command creates a user with the specified username, a home directory (**-m**), and sets the default shell to Bash (**-s /bin/bash**).

- Set Password for the User:

```
$ sudo passwd username
```

You'll be prompted to enter and confirm the password for the user.

Creating System User Accounts

System users are typically used by system services and do not require a home directory or shell.

- Create a System User:

```
$ sudo useradd -r -s /usr/sbin/nologin sysuser
```

The **-r** option creates a system user, and **-s /usr/sbin/nologin** ensures the user cannot log in interactively.

Creating Service User Accounts

Service users are similar to system users but are often associated with specific services or applications.

- Create a Service User:

```
$ sudo useradd -r -m -s /bin/false serviceuser
```

The **-r** option creates a system user, **-m** creates a home directory, and **-s /bin/false** prevents login.

Managing User Accounts

Once user accounts are created, you can manage them using various commands to modify user details, lock/unlock accounts, and delete accounts.

Modifying User Accounts

Use the **usermod** command to change user properties.

- Change User's Shell:

```
$ sudo usermod -s /bin/zsh username
```

This command changes the user's shell to Zsh.

- Change User's Home Directory:

```
$ sudo usermod -d /new/home/dir -m username
```

The **-d** option specifies the new home directory, and **-m** moves the content from the old home directory to the new one.

- Add User to a Group:

```
$ sudo usermod -aG groupname username
```

The **-aG** option appends the user to the specified group.

Locking and Unlocking User Accounts

Lock user accounts to prevent login without deleting them.

- Lock a User Account:

```
$ sudo usermod -L username
```

This command locks the user's password, preventing login.

- Unlock a User Account:

```
$ sudo usermod -U username
```

This command unlocks the user's password, allowing login.

Deleting User Accounts

Use the **userdel** command to remove user accounts.

- Delete a User Account:

```
$ sudo userdel username
```

This command deletes the user account but leaves the home directory and files.

- Delete a User Account and Home Directory:

```
$ sudo userdel -r username
```

The **-r** option removes the user's home directory and files.

Viewing User Account Information

Use the **id**, **finger**, and **getent** commands to view information about user accounts.

- View User ID and Group Information:

```
$ id username
```

This command displays the user's UID, GID, and group memberships.

- Get User Account Details:

```
$ finger username
```

This command displays user information like login name, home directory, and shell.

- Query User Database:

```
$ getent passwd username
```

This command retrieves the user's entry from the **/etc/passwd** file.

Managing User Account Expiry

Set expiry dates for user accounts using the **chage** command.

- Set Account Expiry Date:

```
$ sudo chage -E 2022-12-31 username
```

This command sets the user's account to expire on December 31, 2022.

- View Account Expiry Information:

```
$ chage -l username
```

This command displays the password and account expiry information.

Changing User Password Expiry

Control password expiry policies for users.

- Force Password Change on Next Login:

```
$ sudo chage -d 0 username
```

This command forces the user to change their password on the next login.

- Set Password Expiry Interval:

```
$ sudo chage -M 90 username
```

This command sets the password to expire every 90 days.

Creating Bulk User Accounts

Automate user account creation using a script.

- Create a Script to Add Multiple Users:

Create a file named **add_users.sh**:

```
$ sudo nano add_users.sh
```

Add the following script:

```
#!/bin/bash

for i in {1..10}; do

 username="user$i"

 password="password$i"

 sudo useradd -m -s /bin/bash $username

 echo "$username:$password" | sudo chpasswd

done
```

Save and close the file.

- Make the Script Executable and Run It:

```
$ sudo chmod +x add_users.sh

$ sudo ./add_users.sh
```

This script creates ten user accounts with usernames **user1** to **user10** and sets their passwords.

These scripts and commands will help you manage user accounts on Linux system efficiently, giving each user the rights they need to do their jobs. This method enables you to automate account administration tasks, adjust user preferences, and control their access.

Modifying User Profiles

Modifying user profiles involves changing various attributes of user accounts, such as home directories, shells, group memberships, and more. The **usermod** utility is the primary tool for making these modifications. In this section, we will use **usermod** to modify different types of user profiles created in the previous section.

'Usermod' Overview

The **usermod** command is used to modify existing user accounts in a Linux system. It allows you to change user information such as login names, home directories, shells, group memberships, and account expiry settings.

Using 'usermod'

We shall modify the user profiles for regular users, system users, and service users created in the previous section.

Modifying Regular User Accounts

- Changing the User's Shell:

To change a user's shell, use the **-s** option followed by the path to the new shell.

```
$ sudo usermod -s /bin/zsh user1
```

This command changes **user1**'s shell to Zsh.

- Changing the User's Home Directory:

To change a user's home directory and move their files to the new directory, use the **-d** and **-m** options.

```
$ sudo usermod -d /home/new_user1 -m user1
```

This command sets the new home directory for **user1** to **/home/new_user1** and moves existing files to this directory.

- Adding the User to a New Group:

To add a user to a new group without removing them from other groups, use the **-aG** options.

```
$ sudo usermod -aG sudo user1
```

This command adds **user1** to the **sudo** group.

- Changing the User's Login Name:

To change a user's login name, use the **-l** option followed by the new login name.

```
$ sudo usermod -l newuser1 user1
```

This command changes **user1**'s login name to **newuser1**.

Modifying System User Accounts

- Changing the User's Shell:

System users often have shells set to **/usr/sbin/nologin** or **/bin/false**. To change this:

```
$ sudo usermod -s /bin/bash sysuser
```

This command changes **sysuser**'s shell to Bash, allowing login.

- Locking and Unlocking the User Account:

To lock a system user account, preventing login:

```
$ sudo usermod -L sysuser
```

- To unlock the system user account:

```
$ sudo usermod -U sysuser
```

- Setting an Account Expiry Date:

To set an expiry date for a system user account:

```
$ sudo usermod -e 2023-12-31 sysuser
```

This command sets the expiry date for **sysuser** to December 31, 2023.

Modifying Service User Accounts

- Changing the Home Directory:

Service users might need their home directories changed for configuration purposes.

```
$ sudo usermod -d /srv/new_serviceuser -m serviceuser
```

This command sets the new home directory for **serviceuser** to **/srv/new_serviceuser** and moves existing files.

- Changing the User's Shell:

To ensure a service user cannot log in, set their shell to **/bin/false**.

```
$ sudo usermod -s /bin/false serviceuser
```

- Adding the User to a Specific Group:

If a service user needs to be part of a specific group for permissions:

```
$ sudo usermod -aG www-data serviceuser
```

This command adds **serviceuser** to the **www-data** group.

Viewing Changes Made to User Accounts

After making changes to user accounts, you can view the updated user information using various commands.

- Checking User Information with **getent**:

```
$ getent passwd user1
```

This command retrieves the passwd entry for **user1**, showing updated information such as the home directory and shell.

- Verifying Group Memberships:

```
$ groups user1
```

This command lists all groups that **user1** belongs to.

- Viewing Account Expiry Information with **chage**:

```
$ chage -l sysuser
```

This command displays the password and account expiry information for **sysuser**.

Automating User Modifications

You can automate user modifications using scripts. Given below is a script to batch modify users created previously:

Create a file named **modify_users.sh**:

```
$ sudo nano modify_users.sh
```

Add the following script:

```
#!/bin/bash


for i in {1..10}; do

 username="user$i"

 sudo usermod -s /bin/zsh $username

 sudo usermod -aG sudo $username

 sudo usermod -d /home/new_$username -m $username
```

```
done
```

This script changes the shell to Zsh, adds the user to the **sudo** group, and changes the home directory for users **user1** to **user10**.

Make the Script Executable and Run It:

```
$ sudo chmod +x modify_users.sh

$ sudo ./modify_users.sh
```

This approach ensures that all user modifications are applied consistently across multiple user accounts.

Setting File Permissions and Ownership

File permissions and ownership are crucial in Linux for securing files and directories, ensuring that only authorized users can access or modify them. We shall explore how to define file permissions and ownership for the files and folders created in our AlphaProject, including practical examples.

Understanding File Permissions

In Linux, each file and directory has associated permissions that control read (**r**), write (**w**), and execute (**x**) access for three categories:

1. Owner: The user who owns the file.
2. Group: Users who are part of the file's group.
3. Others: All other users.

Permissions are represented by a string of ten characters, such as **-rwxr-xr--**:

- The first character indicates the type (**-** for a file, **d** for a directory).
- The next three characters (**rwx**) represent permissions for the owner.
- The following three characters (**r-x**) represent permissions for the group.
- The last three characters (**r--**) represent permissions for others.

Setting Permissions with 'chmod'

The **chmod** command is used to change file permissions. Permissions can be set using symbolic (e.g., **r**, **w**, **x**) or numeric (e.g., **755**, **644**) modes.

Using Symbolic Mode

- Granting Read, Write, and Execute Permissions to the Owner:

```
$ chmod u+rwx /projects/AlphaProject
```

- Granting Read and Execute Permissions to the Group:

```
$ chmod g+rx /projects/AlphaProject
```

- Removing Write Permission for Others:

```
$ chmod o-w /projects/AlphaProject
```

Using Numeric Mode

Permissions can also be set using a three-digit octal number, where each digit represents the permissions for owner, group, and others, respectively.

- Setting Permissions to **755** (rwxr-xr-x):

```
$ chmod 755 /projects/AlphaProject
```

- Setting Permissions to **644** (rw-r--r--):

```
$ chmod 644 /projects/AlphaProject/file.txt
```

Changing Ownership with 'chown'

The **chown** command changes the owner and group of a file or directory.

- Changing the Owner of a File:

```
$ sudo chown user1 /projects/AlphaProject/file.txt
```

- Changing the Group of a File:

```
$ sudo chown :developers /projects/AlphaProject/file.txt
```

- Changing Both Owner and Group:

```
$ sudo chown user1:developers
/projects/AlphaProject/file.txt
```

- Changing Ownership Recursively:

```
$ sudo chown -R user1:developers /projects/AlphaProject
```

Sample Program: Setting Permissions and Ownership in AlphaProject

We shall apply these commands to set permissions and ownership for the files and folders created so far in AlphaProject.

- Creating Directories and Files:

```
$ mkdir -p /projects/AlphaProject/{src,bin,logs}

$ touch
/projects/AlphaProject/{README.md,src/main.py,logs/app.lo
g}
```

- Setting Directory Permissions:

Set directory permissions to allow the owner full access, the group read and execute access, and others no access:

```
$ chmod 750 /projects/AlphaProject

$ chmod 750 /projects/AlphaProject/src

$ chmod 750 /projects/AlphaProject/bin

$ chmod 750 /projects/AlphaProject/logs
```

- Setting File Permissions:

Set file permissions to allow the owner read and write access, the group read access, and others no access:

```
$ chmod 640 /projects/AlphaProject/README.md
$ chmod 640 /projects/AlphaProject/src/main.py
$ chmod 640 /projects/AlphaProject/logs/app.log
```

Setting Ownership:

Change the ownership of the project files to user1 and the developers group:

```
$ sudo chown -R user1:developers /projects/AlphaProject
```

- Verifying Permissions and Ownership:

List the directory to verify permissions and ownership:

```
$ ls -l /projects/AlphaProject
```

Desired output:

```
drwxr-x--- 3 user1 developers 4096 Jan 1 12:00 bin
drwxr-x--- 3 user1 developers 4096 Jan 1 12:00 logs
drwxr-x--- 3 user1 developers 4096 Jan 1 12:00 src
-rw-r----- 1 user1 developers 0 Jan 1 12:00 README.md
```

Using 'umask' to Set Default Permissions

The **umask** command sets default permissions for newly created files and directories. It defines which permission bits will not be set.

- Viewing the Current **umask**:

```
$ umask
```

- Setting a **umask**:

To set a default **umask** that allows read and write permissions for the owner, and read permissions for the group, use:

```
$ umask 022
```

- Persistent **umask** Setting:

To make the **umask** setting persistent, add it to the user's shell configuration file (e.g., **~/.bashrc**):

```
echo "umask 022" >> ~/.bashrc

source ~/.bashrc
```

Advanced Permissions with Setuid, Setgid, and Sticky Bit

Setuid

Setuid (Set User ID) allows a file to be executed with the privileges of the file's owner.

- Setting Setuid:

```
$ sudo chmod u+s /projects/AlphaProject/bin/script.sh
```

Setgid

Setgid (Set Group ID) allows a file to be executed with the privileges of the file's group, and directories created within a setgid directory inherit the group of the directory.

- Setting Setgid on a Directory:

```
$ sudo chmod g+s /projects/AlphaProject/src
```

Sticky Bit

The sticky bit on a directory restricts file deletion; only the file owner, directory owner, and root can delete or rename files.

- Setting Sticky Bit:

```
$ sudo chmod +t /projects/AlphaProject/logs
```

Sample Program: Advanced Permissions

Creating a Script with Setuid

- Create a script in the **bin** directory:

```
$ echo -e '#!/bin/bash\necho "Running as $(whoami)"' >
/projects/AlphaProject/bin/script.sh

$ chmod +x /projects/AlphaProject/bin/script.sh
```

- Setting Setuid on the Script:

```
$ sudo chmod u+s /projects/AlphaProject/bin/script.sh
```

Testing the Script

- Execute the script as a different user:

```
$ sudo -u user2 /projects/AlphaProject/bin/script.sh
```

The script runs with **user1**'s privileges.

- Creating a Directory with Setgid:

```
$ mkdir /projects/AlphaProject/shared

$ sudo chmod g+s /projects/AlphaProject/shared
```

Creating Files in Setgid Directory

Files created in the **shared** directory inherit the group **developers**:

```
$ touch /projects/AlphaProject/shared/file.txt

$ ls -l /projects/AlphaProject/shared/file.txt
```

- Setting Sticky Bit on the Logs Directory:

```
$ sudo chmod +t /projects/AlphaProject/logs
```

Verifying Sticky Bit

The sticky bit ensures only the owner can delete files in the **logs** directory:

```
$ ls -ld /projects/AlphaProject/logs
```

AlphaProject's file permissions and ownership can be efficiently managed through the configuration of these settings and commands. This method gives you a thorough grasp of Linux file permission management by covering everything from fundamental permission settings to sophisticated permission procedures, including ownership changes.

Using ACLs (Access Control Lists)

Introduction to ACLs

ACLs provide a more flexible permission mechanism for files and directories in Linux compared to the traditional Unix permission model. ACLs allow you to define permissions for multiple users and groups, beyond the basic owner-group-other categories.

An ACL specifies which users or system processes can access specific resources, as well as what operations they can perform. ACLs extend the standard file permission model by allowing you to set permissions for any number of users and groups on a per-file or per-directory basis.

Key Concepts of ACLs:

- ACL Entries: Each ACL entry defines the permissions for a specific user or group.
- Access ACLs: Apply to files and directories, specifying permissions for reading, writing, and executing.
- Default ACLs: Apply to directories, specifying the default permissions for newly created files and subdirectories within the directory.

Configuring ACLs

To work with ACLs, ensure the filesystem supports ACLs (e.g., ext4, XFS) and the **acl** package is installed.

- Install the ACL Package:

```
$ sudo apt install acl
```

- Enable ACLs on the Filesystem (if not enabled by default):
    - Mount the filesystem with the **acl** option:

```
$ sudo mount -o remount,acl /dev/sda1 /mnt
```

- To make this change permanent, add the **acl** option to **/etc/fstab**:

```
$ sudo nano /etc/fstab
```

- Add **acl** to the relevant line:

```
/dev/sda1 /mnt ext4 defaults,acl 0 0
```

Sample Program: Using ACLs in AlphaProject

- At first, setup the Project Directory:

```
$ mkdir -p /projects/AlphaProject/{src,bin,logs}

$ sudo chown -R user1:developers /projects/AlphaProject

$ sudo chmod -R 750 /projects/AlphaProject
```

- Set ACLs for Specific Users:

Use **setfacl** to set ACLs. For example, allow **user2** to read and write to the **src** directory:

```
$ sudo setfacl -m u:user2:rw /projects/AlphaProject/src
```

- Verify the ACL:

Use **getfacl** to view the ACLs of a file or directory:

```
$ getfacl /projects/AlphaProject/src
```

Desired output:

```
# file: projects/AlphaProject/src

# owner: user1

# group: developers

user::rwx

user:user2:rw-

group::r-x

mask::rwx

other::---
```

- Set Default ACLs:

Default ACLs ensure that new files and directories inherit the ACLs from their parent directory. For example, set default ACLs on the **logs** directory:

```
$ sudo setfacl -d -m u:user2:rw
/projects/AlphaProject/logs
```

- Verify the default ACL:

```
$ getfacl /projects/AlphaProject/logs
```

Desired output:

```
# file: projects/AlphaProject/logs

# owner: user1

# group: developers

user::rwx

group::r-x
```

```
other::---
default:user::rwx
default:user:user2:rw-
default:group::r-x
default:mask::rwx
default:other::---
```

Scenario 1: Granting Temporary Write Access

Suppose **user3** needs temporary write access to the **src** directory to help with development.

- Grant Write Access:

```
$ sudo setfacl -m u:user3:rw /projects/AlphaProject/src
```

- Remove Write Access After Completion:

```
$ sudo setfacl -x u:user3 /projects/AlphaProject/src
```

Scenario 2: Providing Read-Only Access to Logs

user4 needs read-only access to the **logs** directory to monitor application logs.

- Grant Read-Only Access:

```
$ sudo setfacl -m u:user4:r /projects/AlphaProject/logs
```

Scenario 3: Inheriting Permissions for New Files

Ensure that any new files created in the **src** directory have specific permissions for **user2**.

- Set Default ACLs:

```
$ sudo setfacl -d -m u:user2:rw
/projects/AlphaProject/src
```

- Verify the Inheritance:

Create a new file and check its ACL:

```
$ touch /projects/AlphaProject/src/newfile.txt

$ getfacl /projects/AlphaProject/src/newfile.txt
```

Desired output:

```
# file: projects/AlphaProject/src/newfile.txt

# owner: user1

# group: developers

user::rw-

user:user2:rw-

group::r-x

mask::rw-

other::---
```

Scenario 4: Masking ACL Permissions

The mask controls the maximum effective permissions for all entries except the owner. Suppose you want to restrict all additional users to read-only access in the **logs** directory, regardless of their individual ACL entries.

- Set the Mask:

```
$ sudo setfacl -m m::r /projects/AlphaProject/logs
```

- Verify the Mask:

```
$ getfacl /projects/AlphaProject/logs
```

Desired output:

```
# file: projects/AlphaProject/logs
# owner: user1
# group: developers
user::rwx
user:user2:rw-
group::r-x
mask::r--
other::---
default:user::rwx
default:user:user2:rw-
default:group::r-x
default:mask::r--
default:other::---
```

Scenario 5: Removing All ACL Entries

If you decide to revert to standard permissions and remove all ACL entries for a file or directory:

- Remove ACLs:

```
$ sudo setfacl -b /projects/AlphaProject/src
```

- Verify Removal:

```
$ getfacl /projects/AlphaProject/src
```

The output should no longer show any additional ACL entries.

This approach ensures that multiple users and groups have the appropriate permissions to perform their tasks without compromising the overall security and integrity of the AlphaProject

Managing User Sessions

For activity monitoring, system security, and resource availability, managing user sessions is extremely important. This section will go over the key elements of session management in a Linux environment, including how to detect, monitor, and finally end user sessions.

Identifying User Sessions

To manage user sessions, you first need to identify which users are logged into the system and gather details about their sessions.

Using 'who'

The **who** command displays a list of users currently logged into the system.

```
$ who
```

Desired output:

```
user1 tty7 2024-05-20 10:00 (:0)

user2 pts/0 2024-05-20 10:05 (192.168.1.10)

user3 pts/1 2024-05-20 10:10 (192.168.1.11)
```

This output shows the username, terminal, login time, and remote host (if applicable).

Using 'w'

The **w** command provides more detailed information about logged-in users and their activities.

```
$ w
```

Desired output:

```
10:15:32 up 2:15, 3 users, load average: 0.25, 0.30, 0.25

USER TTY FROM LOGIN@ IDLE JCPU PCPU WHAT

user1 tty7 :0 10:00 2:15m 0.10s 0.10s /usr/bin/gnome-
session
```

```
user2 pts/0 192.168.1.10 10:05 0.01s 0.20s 0.05s bash

user3 pts/1 192.168.1.11 10:10 0.02s 0.15s 0.03s sshd:
user3 [priv]
```

This output includes the idle time, JCPU (time used by all processes attached to the tty), and PCPU (time used by the current process).

Using 'last'

The **last** command shows the history of user logins.

```
$ last
```

Desired output:

```
user3 pts/1 192.168.1.11 Mon May 20 10:10 still logged in

user2 pts/0 192.168.1.10 Mon May 20 10:05 still logged in

user1 tty7 :0 Mon May 20 10:00 still logged in

reboot system boot 5.4.0-42-generic Mon May 20 08:00
still running
```

This output shows the user logins, login times, and logout times.

Tracking User Sessions

Tracking user sessions involves monitoring user activities and gathering detailed session information.

Using 'ps'

The **ps** command displays information about active processes. You can use it to track processes started by a specific user.

```
$ ps -u user2
```

Desired output:

```
PID TTY TIME CMD
 1350 pts/0 00:00:00 bash
 1365 pts/0 00:00:00 ps
```

This command shows the processes started by **user2**.

Using 'top'

The **top** command provides a dynamic, real-time view of running processes, including user sessions.

```
$ top -u user2
```

This command filters the output to show only the processes owned by **user2**.

Using 'htop'

The **htop** command is an enhanced version of **top** with a more user-friendly interface. To filter by user:

```
$ htop
```

Press **F4** and type the username to filter the processes by that user.

Suspending User Sessions

Suspending a user session involves pausing all processes associated with the session without terminating them. This can be done using signals.

Using 'kill -STOP'

The **kill -STOP** command sends a STOP signal to suspend a process.

- Find the PID:

```
$ ps -u user2
```

- Suspend the Process:

```
$ sudo kill -STOP 1350
```

Using 'pkill'

The **pkill** command can send signals to processes based on criteria such as username.

```
$ sudo pkill -STOP -u user2
```

This command suspends all processes belonging to **user2**.

Resuming User Sessions

Resuming a user session involves sending a CONT signal to continue the suspended processes.

Using 'kill -CONT'

- Find the PID:

```
$ ps -u user2
```

- Resume the Process:

```
$ sudo kill -CONT 1350
```

Using 'pkill'

```
$ sudo pkill -CONT -u user2
```

This command resumes all processes belonging to **user2**.

Terminating User Sessions

Terminating a user session involves stopping all processes associated with the session.

Using 'kill'

The **kill** command sends signals to processes to terminate them.

- Find the PID:

```
$ ps -u user2
```

- Terminate the Process:

```
$ sudo kill -TERM 1350
```

Using 'pkill'

The **pkill** command can be used to terminate all processes for a user.

```
$ sudo pkill -TERM -u user2
```

Using 'killall'

The **killall** command kills all instances of a specified process.

```
$ sudo killall -u user2
```

This command terminates all processes belonging to **user2**.

Using 'skill'

The **skill** command sends a signal to all processes owned by a specific user.

```
$ sudo skill -KILL -u user2
```

This command forcefully kills all processes owned by **user2**.

Sample Program: Managing User Sessions in AlphaProject

Scenario 1: Identifying and Tracking User Sessions

- List Currently Logged-In Users:

```
$ who
```

- Detailed Information on User Sessions:

```
$ w
```

- View User Login History:

```
$ last
```

- Monitor Processes for a Specific User:

```
$ ps -u user2
$ top -u user2
```

Scenario 2: Suspending and Resuming Sessions

- Suspend All Processes for **user2**:

```
$ sudo pkill -STOP -u user2
```

- Verify Suspension:

```
$ ps -u user2
```

- Resume All Processes for **user2**:

```
$ sudo pkill -CONT -u user2
```

- Verify Resumption:

```
$ ps -u user2
```

Scenario 3: Terminating User Sessions

- Terminate All Processes for **user2**:

```
$ sudo pkill -TERM -u user2
```

- Verify Termination:

```
$ ps -u user2
```

- Forcefully Kill All Processes for **user2**:

```
$ sudo skill -KILL -u user2
```

- Verify All Processes Are Terminated:

```
$ ps -u user2
```

Gaining proficiency in these commands and procedures will allow you to efficiently manage user sessions and a full command over user actions on the system and includes locating, following, pausing, and ending user sessions.

Configuring 'sudo' for Administrative Tasks

sudo (superuser do) is a command-line utility that allows a permitted user to execute a command as the superuser or another user, as specified by the security policy. Configuring **sudo** is crucial for delegating administrative tasks without giving users full root access, thereby enhancing system security and accountability.

Necessity of Configuring 'sudo'

Configuring **sudo** is essential for several reasons:

1. Limits the use of the root account, reducing the risk of accidental or malicious system changes.
2. Logs the commands executed by users with elevated privileges, providing an audit trail.
3. Grants specific administrative privileges to users or groups, allowing them to perform necessary tasks without full administrative rights.

Configuring 'sudo'

To configure **sudo**, you edit the **/etc/sudoers** file using the **visudo** command, which ensures syntax correctness and prevents multiple simultaneous edits.

- Open the **sudoers** File with **visudo**:

```
$ sudo visudo
```

- Adding a User to the **sudo** Group:

The **sudo** group is a common way to grant users administrative privileges.

```
$ sudo usermod -aG sudo username
```

Users in the **sudo** group can execute any command as root.

You can grant specific permissions to users or groups. For example, to allow **user2** to restart the **apache2** service:

```
user2 ALL=(ALL) NOPASSWD: /bin/systemctl restart apache2
```

This entry allows **user2** to restart **apache2** without needing a password.

Sample Program: Using 'sudo'

Scenario 1: Basic Administrative Tasks

Users need elevated privileges to update the system. Granting **user2** permission to update the system:

```
user2 ALL=(ALL) NOPASSWD: /usr/bin/apt update,
/usr/bin/apt upgrade
```

Now, **user2** can run:

```
$ sudo apt update

$ sudo apt upgrade
```

To allow **user2** to start and stop the **apache2** service:

```
user2 ALL=(ALL) NOPASSWD: /bin/systemctl start apache2,
/bin/systemctl stop apache2

$ sudo systemctl start apache2

$ sudo systemctl stop apache2
```

Scenario 2: User Management

To allow **user2** to add new users:

```
user2 ALL=(ALL) NOPASSWD: /usr/sbin/useradd

$ sudo useradd newuser
```

To allow **user2** to change passwords for other users:

```
user2 ALL=(ALL) NOPASSWD: /usr/bin/passwd

$ sudo passwd otheruser
```

Scenario 3: File and Directory Management

To allow **user2** to edit the **/etc/apache2/apache2.conf** file:

```
user2 ALL=(ALL) NOPASSWD: /usr/bin/nano
/etc/apache2/apache2.conf

$ sudo nano /etc/apache2/apache2.conf
```

To allow **user2** to manage files in **/projects/AlphaProject**:

```
user2 ALL=(ALL) NOPASSWD: /bin/chown, /bin/chmod,
/bin/rm, /bin/mv, /bin/cp, /bin/mkdir

$ sudo chown user2:developers /projects/AlphaProject/*

$ sudo chmod 755 /projects/AlphaProject/newfile

$ sudo rm /projects/AlphaProject/oldfile

$ sudo mv /projects/AlphaProject/file1
/projects/AlphaProject/dir/

$ sudo cp /projects/AlphaProject/file2
/projects/AlphaProject/backup/
```

```
$ sudo mkdir /projects/AlphaProject/newdir
```

Scenario 4: Network Management

To allow **user2** to manage network interfaces:

```
user2 ALL=(ALL) NOPASSWD: /sbin/ifconfig, /sbin/ip

$ sudo ifconfig eth0 up

$ sudo ip addr add 192.168.1.10/24 dev eth0
```

To allow **user2** to manage **iptables**:

```
user2 ALL=(ALL) NOPASSWD: /sbin/iptables

$ sudo iptables -L

$ sudo iptables -A INPUT -p tcp --dport 22 -j ACCEPT
```

Scenario 5: System Monitoring

To allow **user2** to view system logs:

```
user2 ALL=(ALL) NOPASSWD: /usr/bin/tail -f
/var/log/syslog, /usr/bin/tail -f /var/log/auth.log

$ sudo tail -f /var/log/syslog

$ sudo tail -f /var/log/auth.log
```

To allow **user2** to use performance monitoring tools:

```
user2 ALL=(ALL) NOPASSWD: /usr/bin/top, /usr/bin/htop,
/usr/bin/iostat

$ sudo top
```

```
$ sudo htop

$ sudo iostat
```

Scenario 6: Limiting Command Execution

To restrict **user2** to only restart **apache2**:

```
Cmnd_Alias APACHE_RESTART = /bin/systemctl restart
apache2

user2 ALL=(ALL) NOPASSWD: APACHE_RESTART

$ sudo systemctl restart apache2
```

To allow **user2** to run commands only on a specific host:

```
user2 myhostname=(ALL) NOPASSWD: /usr/bin/passwd

$ sudo passwd user3
```

Scenario 7: Using Aliases

To simplify the sudoers file, define command aliases:

```
Cmnd_Alias NETWORK_CMDS = /sbin/ifconfig, /sbin/ip

Cmnd_Alias SYSTEM_CMDS = /usr/bin/apt update,
/usr/bin/apt upgrade

user2 ALL=(ALL) NOPASSWD: NETWORK_CMDS, SYSTEM_CMDS

$ sudo ifconfig eth0 up

$ sudo apt update
```

To group users with similar permissions:

```
User_Alias ADMINS = user2, user3
```

```
ADMINS ALL=(ALL) NOPASSWD: ALL

$ sudo systemctl restart apache2
```

Scenario 8: Including External Files

To include configuration from external files:

```
# In /etc/sudoers

@includedir /etc/sudoers.d
```

Create a file in **/etc/sudoers.d** for **user2**:

```
$ sudo nano /etc/sudoers.d/user2
```

Add the permissions:

```
user2 ALL=(ALL) NOPASSWD: /bin/systemctl restart apache2
```

Gaining expertise with **sudo** configuration and usage allows you to swiftly and safely delegate administrative tasks to users, giving them the rights they need to accomplish their jobs while keeping the system secure and monitoring their activity.

Password Policies and Management

Users are more likely to generate secure, unique passwords if strict password regulations are in place. In this section, we'll learn methods to safeguard user passwords, determine AlphaProject's password regulations, and put them into action.

Establishing Password Policies

To enforce password policies, we will use the **pam_pwquality** module, which is part of the Pluggable Authentication Modules (PAM) framework. This module allows you to set requirements for password strength and complexity.

Step 1: Install 'pam_pwquality'

First, ensure that the **pam_pwquality** package is installed:

```
$ sudo apt install libpam-pwquality
```

Step 2: Configure 'pam_pwquality'

- Edit the PAM configuration file for password management:

```
$ sudo nano /etc/pam.d/common-password
```

- Add or modify the following line to include **pam_pwquality**:

```
password requisite pam_pwquality.so retry=3 minlen=12
dcredit=-1 ucredit=-1 ocredit=-1 lcredit=-1
```

- **retry=3**: Allows three attempts to enter a valid password.
- **minlen=12**: Sets the minimum password length to 12 characters.
- **dcredit=-1**: Requires at least one digit.
- **ucredit=-1**: Requires at least one uppercase letter.
- **ocredit=-1**: Requires at least one special character.
- **lcredit=-1**: Requires at least one lowercase letter.

Step 3: Enforcing Password Expiration

- To enforce password expiration policies, edit the **/etc/login.defs** file:

```
$ sudo nano /etc/login.defs
```

- Add or modify the following lines:

```
PASS_MAX_DAYS 90

PASS_MIN_DAYS 7

PASS_WARN_AGE 14
```

- **PASS_MAX_DAYS**: Maximum number of days a password is valid (90 days).

- **PASS_MIN_DAYS**: Minimum number of days between password changes (7 days).
- **PASS_WARN_AGE**: Number of days before password expiration to warn users (14 days).

Step 4: Applying Password Policies to Existing Users

Use the **chage** command to apply policies to existing users:

```
$ sudo chage -M 90 -m 7 -W 14 user1

$ sudo chage -M 90 -m 7 -W 14 user2
```

Securing Passwords

Step 1: Use Strong Hashing Algorithms

Ensure that passwords are hashed using strong algorithms. Edit the **/etc/login.defs** file to specify the hashing algorithm:

```
ENCRYPT_METHOD SHA512
```

Step 2: Restrict Access to Password Files

Verify that the **/etc/shadow** file, which stores hashed passwords, has the correct permissions:

```
$ ls -l /etc/shadow
```

The output should show that only the root user has read and write access:

```
-rw-r----- 1 root shadow 1523 May 20 10:00 /etc/shadow
```

Step 3: Use 'chpasswd' for Batch Password Updates

If you need to update passwords in bulk, use the **chpasswd** command, which reads a list of username-password pairs from a file:

- Create a File with Username-Password Pairs:

```
$ sudo nano /tmp/users.txt
```

- Add the following content:

```
user1:newpassword1

user2:newpassword2
```

- Update Passwords:

```
$ sudo chpasswd < /tmp/users.txt
```

Step 4: Enforce Password History

To prevent users from reusing old passwords, configure the **pam_unix** module. Edit the PAM configuration file for password management:

```
$ sudo nano /etc/pam.d/common-password
```

Add or modify the following line to include **remember**:

```
password [success=1 default=ignore] pam_unix.so obscure
use_authtok try_first_pass yescrypt remember=5
```

This configuration ensures that the last five passwords cannot be reused.

Sample Program: Enforcing Password Policy and Management

Scenario 1: Enforcing Password Complexity

Install and Configure **pam_pwquality**:

```
$ sudo apt install libpam-pwquality

$ sudo nano /etc/pam.d/common-password
```

Add the line:

```
password requisite pam_pwquality.so retry=3 minlen=12
dcredit=-1 ucredit=-1 ocredit=-1 lcredit=-1
```

Attempt to change a password with insufficient complexity:

```
$ sudo passwd user1
```

Enter a weak password and observe the rejection, then enter a strong password to meet the criteria.

Scenario 2: Implementing Password Expiration Policies

Configure Expiration Policies:

```
$ sudo nano /etc/login.defs
```

Add or modify the lines:

```
PASS_MAX_DAYS 90

PASS_MIN_DAYS 7

PASS_WARN_AGE 14
```

Apply Policies to Existing Users:

```
$ sudo chage -M 90 -m 7 -W 14 user1
```

Scenario 3: Ensuring Secure Password Storage

Verify Password File Permissions:

```
$ ls -l /etc/shadow
```

Ensure the output shows:

```
-rw-r----- 1 root shadow 1523 May 20 10:00 /etc/shadow
```

Set Strong Hashing Algorithm:

```
$ sudo nano /etc/login.defs
```

Add or modify the line:

```
ENCRYPT_METHOD SHA512
```

Scenario 4: Batch Updating Passwords

Create a File with Username-Password Pairs:

```
$ sudo nano /tmp/users.txt
```

Add the following content:

```
user1:newpassword1

user2:newpassword2
```

Update Passwords:

```
$ sudo chpasswd < /tmp/users.txt
```

Scenario 5: Preventing Password Reuse

Configure **pam_unix** for Password History:

```
$ sudo nano /etc/pam.d/common-password
```

Add or modify the line:

```
password [success=1 default=ignore] pam_unix.so obscure
use_authtok try_first_pass yescrypt remember=5
```

This method improves system security by lowering the likelihood of unwanted access and making sure passwords are strong, unique, and protected.

Working with PAM (Pluggable Authentication Modules)

PAM Overview

Pluggable Authentication Modules (PAM) provide a flexible mechanism for authenticating users in Linux. PAM is a suite of shared libraries that enable the local system administrator to choose how applications authenticate users. PAM modules can be stacked to create comprehensive authentication policies.

The primary purpose of PAM is to provide a common authentication framework for Linux applications. It allows administrators to:

1. Use a consistent authentication mechanism across multiple applications.
2. Easily configure and change authentication methods without modifying application code.
3. Implement various security policies, such as account lockout, password policies, and multi-factor authentication.

Setting up PAM

PAM configuration files are located in **/etc/pam.d/**. Each file corresponds to a specific application or service. The configuration files consist of directives that include module-type, control-flag, module-path, and module-arguments.

Sample of PAM Configuration File Structure:

```
module-type control-flag module-path module-arguments
```

In the above config file,

1. Module-Type: Defines the type of PAM function (e.g., **auth**, **account**, **password**, **session**).
2. Control-Flag: Determines the action on module success or failure (**required**, **requisite**, **sufficient**, **optional**).
3. Module-Path: Path to the PAM module (e.g., **/lib/security/pam_unix.so**).
4. Module-Arguments: Arguments passed to the PAM module (e.g., **try_first_pass**).

Sample Program: PAM Configuration

Example 1: Basic Authentication with pam_unix

The **pam_unix** module handles traditional UNIX authentication, which includes verifying passwords against **/etc/passwd** and **/etc/shadow**.

Edit the **/etc/pam.d/login** file:

```
$ sudo nano /etc/pam.d/login
```

Add or ensure the following lines are present:

```
auth required pam_env.so

auth required pam_unix.so

account required pam_unix.so

password required pam_unix.so

session required pam_unix.so
```

In the above example,

1. **auth required pam_env.so**: Initializes the environment variables.
2. **auth required pam_unix.so**: Uses UNIX authentication to verify the user's password.
3. **account required pam_unix.so**: Checks the validity of the account.
4. **password required pam_unix.so**: Handles password changes.
5. **session required pam_unix.so**: Manages session settings.

Example 2: Enabling MFA with 'pam_google_authenticator'

Multi-factor authentication(MFA) adds an extra layer of security by requiring a second form of authentication.

- Install Google Authenticator:

```
$ sudo apt install libpam-google-authenticator
```

- Configure PAM for SSH:

Edit the **/etc/pam.d/sshd** file:

```
$ sudo nano /etc/pam.d/sshd
```

Add the following line:

```
auth required pam_google_authenticator.so
```

- Configure SSHD:

Edit the **/etc/ssh/sshd_config** file:

```
$ sudo nano /etc/ssh/sshd_config
```

Ensure the following lines are present:

```
ChallengeResponseAuthentication yes
```

- Restart SSH Service:

```
$ sudo systemctl restart sshd
```

- Setup Google Authenticator for a User:

Log in as the user and run:

```
$ google-authenticator
```

Follow the prompts to configure the Google Authenticator.

Example 3: Restricting Login Times with 'pam_time'

The **pam_time** module allows you to restrict user logins based on time and day.

- Configure **pam_time** in Login:

Edit the **/etc/pam.d/login** file:

```
$ sudo nano /etc/pam.d/login
```

Add the following line:

```
account required pam_time.so
```

- Configure Time Restrictions:

Edit the **/etc/security/time.conf** file:

```
$ sudo nano /etc/security/time.conf
```

Add the following rule to restrict **user1** to log in only during weekdays from 9 AM to 5 PM:

```
login; *; user1; MoTuWeThFr0900-1700
```

Example 4: Enforcing Password Complexity with 'pam_pwquality'

Configure **pam_pwquality**:

Edit the **/etc/pam.d/common-password** file:

```
$ sudo nano /etc/pam.d/common-password
```

Add or modify the following line:

```
password requisite pam_pwquality.so retry=3 minlen=12
dcredit=-1 ucredit=-1 ocredit=-1 lcredit=-1
```

Sample Program: Managing PAM for AlphaProject

To manage PAM effectively for AlphaProject, you need to implement and customize PAM configurations for various scenarios.

Scenario 1: Protecting SSH Access

- Configure SSH Authentication:

Edit the **/etc/pam.d/sshd** file:

```
$ sudo nano /etc/pam.d/sshd
```

Add the following lines to enable multi-factor authentication and enforce password complexity:

```
auth required pam_google_authenticator.so
```

```
auth required pam_pwquality.so retry=3 minlen=12
dcredit=-1 ucredit=-1 ocredit=-1 lcredit=-1
```

- Configure SSHD:

Edit the **/etc/ssh/sshd_config** file:

```
$ sudo nano /etc/ssh/sshd_config
```

Ensure these settings:

```
ChallengeResponseAuthentication yes

PasswordAuthentication yes
```

- Restart SSH Service:

```
$ sudo systemctl restart sshd
```

Scenario 2: Restricting Login Times for Developers

- Configure Login Time Restrictions:

Edit the **/etc/pam.d/login** file:

```
$ sudo nano /etc/pam.d/login
```

Add:

```
account required pam_time.so
```

- Set Time Restrictions:

Edit the **/etc/security/time.conf** file:

```
$ sudo nano /etc/security/time.conf
```

Add rules to restrict developer logins to working hours:

```
login; *; user2; MoTuWeThFr0900-1700

login; *; user3; MoTuWeThFr0900-1700
```

Scenario 3: Enforcing Account Lockout After Failed Attempts

The **pam_tally2** module can lock user accounts after a number of failed login attempts.

- Install **pam_tally2**:

```
$ sudo apt install libpam-modules
```

- Configure Account Lockout:

Edit the **/etc/pam.d/common-auth** file:

```
$ sudo nano /etc/pam.d/common-auth
```

Add the following lines:

```
auth required pam_tally2.so deny=5 onerr=fail
unlock_time=600

account required pam_tally2.so
```

In the above snippet,

  - **deny=5**: Locks account after 5 failed attempts.
  - **unlock_time=600**: Automatically unlocks account after 10 minutes.

- View Failed Attempts:

To check the number of failed login attempts for a user:

```
$ sudo pam_tally2 --user user1
```

- Reset Failed Attempt Counter:

To reset the counter for a user:

```
$ sudo pam_tally2 --user user1 --reset
```

These PAM setups will help you handle the authentication processes of AlphaProject and improve its security. By taking this route, you may rest assured that your project's authentication system will be adaptable, safe, and strong.

Managing Group Memberships

Overview

Group memberships in Linux are an essential part of managing user permissions and access control. Groups allow you to assign a set of permissions to multiple users, simplifying the administration of file permissions, application access, and more.

Group memberships are defined and stored in the **/etc/group** file. This file contains information about all groups and their members in a Linux system.

Each line in the **/etc/group** file represents a group and has the following format:

```
group_name:x:GID:user1,user2,user3
```

where,

- **group_name**: The name of the group.
- **x**: Placeholder for the password field (usually not used).
- **GID**: The Group ID number.
- **user1,user2,user3**: A comma-separated list of users who are members of the group.

Managing Group Memberships

Managing group memberships involves creating groups, adding users to groups, removing users from groups, and modifying group properties.

Creating Groups

Groups can be created using the **groupadd** command.

Create a New Group:

```
$ sudo groupadd developers
```

This command creates a new group named **developers**.

Adding Users to Groups

Users can be added to groups using the **usermod** command or directly editing the **/etc/group** file.

Add a User to a Group:

```
$ sudo usermod -aG developers user1
```

This command adds **user1** to the **developers** group without removing them from other groups.

Removing Users from Groups

Users can be removed from groups using the **gpasswd** command or by editing the **/etc/group** file.

Remove a User from a Group:

```
$ sudo gpasswd -d user1 developers
```

This command removes **user1** from the **developers** group.

Modifying Group Properties

Group properties, such as the group name and GID, can be modified using the **groupmod** command.

- Change the Group Name:

```
$ sudo groupmod -n devteam developers
```

This command changes the name of the **developers** group to **devteam**.

- Change the Group ID:

```
$ sudo groupmod -g 1001 devteam
```

This command changes the GID of the **devteam** group to **1001**.

Sample Program: Managing Group Memberships in AlphaProject

Scenario 1: Setting up Initial Group Memberships

For AlphaProject, we need to create a group for developers and assign users to this group.

- Create the **developers** Group:

```
$ sudo groupadd developers
```

- Add Users to the **developers** Group:

```
$ sudo usermod -aG developers user1

$ sudo usermod -aG developers user2

$ sudo usermod -aG developers user3
```

Scenario 2: Managing Access for a New Team Member

When a new developer, **user4**, joins the project, they need to be added to the **developers** group.

Add **user4** to the **developers** Group:

```
$ sudo usermod -aG developers user4
```

Scenario 3: Removing a Developer from the Project

If a developer, **user2**, leaves the project, they need to be removed from the **developers** group.

Remove **user2** from the **developers** Group:

```
$ sudo gpasswd -d user2 developers
```

Scenario 4: Creating and Managing Additional Groups

Suppose we need a separate group for administrators who have elevated privileges.

- Create the **admins** Group:

```
$ sudo groupadd admins
```

- Add Users to the **admins** Group:

```
$ sudo usermod -aG admins user1

$ sudo usermod -aG admins user3
```

- Verify Group Memberships:

Use the **groups** command to check the groups a user belongs to:

```
$ groups user1

$ groups user3
```

Scenario 5: Modifying Group Information

If we decide to rename the **developers** group to **devteam** for better clarity:

- Rename the **developers** Group:

```
$ sudo groupmod -n devteam developers
```

- Verify the Change:

Check the **/etc/group** file to ensure the group name has been updated:

```
$ grep 'devteam' /etc/group
```

Scenario 6: Setting Group Ownership on Directories

To ensure that all files created in the **/projects/AlphaProject** directory belong to the **developers** group:

- Change the Group Ownership:

```
$ sudo chown -R :developers /projects/AlphaProject
```

- Set the SGID Bit:

This ensures that new files and subdirectories inherit the group ownership of the parent directory:

```
$ sudo chmod g+s /projects/AlphaProject
```

- Verify the Permissions:

List the directory to verify the SGID bit:

```
$ ls -ld /projects/AlphaProject
```

Scenario 7: Managing Group Memberships Directly in /etc/group

While command-line tools are the recommended way to manage group memberships, you can also directly edit the **/etc/group** file for quick changes.

- Edit the **/etc/group** File:

```
$ sudo nano /etc/group
```

- Add or modify the line for the **developers** group:

```
developers:x:1001:user1,user3,user4
```

- Use the **getent** command to verify the group information:

```
$ getent group developers
```

You can manage who has access to what in AlphaProject and make sure everyone has the rights they need by keeping track of group memberships. In addition to improving the safety and structure of your project environment, this method streamlines the process of managing user rights.

Summary

The concluding chapter of this book explored the administration of users and permissions in Linux. The first part of the chapter covered managing user accounts, which included making use of commands like useradd and usermod to create different kinds of user accounts. Some of the methods tested for profile modification included altering user shells, home directories, and group memberships. To offer finer-grained permissions than the conventional user-group-other approach, Access Control Lists (ACLs) were implemented. ACLs were configured, viewed, and modified for particular users and scenarios through the use of particular instances.

Another significant topic was managing user sessions, which involved using commands such as who, w, and last to identify and track user sessions. We went over how to use kill, pkill, and skill to pause, resume, and end user sessions. We covered why sudo configuration is essential for admin activities, and we looked at how to set up sudo policies in the /etc/sudoers file and how to grant users certain access.

To handle password rules and administration, we used pam pwquality to set complexity criteria, enforce password expiration standards, and secure password storage. Also learned were methods for avoiding password reuse and upgrading passwords in bulk.

This chapter also provided a comprehensive overview of Pluggable Authentication Modules (PAM), outlining its function and showing how to configure various authentication methods. Users were given the option to configure several security features, such as pam_google_authenticator for multi-factor authentication, pam_time for time restrictions on logins, and pam_tally2 for account lockout.

Last but not least, we looked at group membership management, including the storage location of group memberships and the commands groupadd, usermod, gpasswd, and groupmod for creating, editing, and deleting groups.

Index

A

B

C

D

E

F

G

H

I

K

L

M

N

P

R

S

T

U

V

W

Y

Epilogue

As you near the end of "Linux Basics for SysAdmin," you've made tremendous progress in understanding the fundamental skills required for effective Linux system management. This book has given you a thorough grasp of the Linux operating system, its command line interface, and the many tools and commands required to administer business systems on an essential level.

From exploring the Linux filesystem and using basic commands to managing users, permissions, and processes, you've laid a solid basis for any system administrator. You've learned how to install and manage software and hardware, configure services, measure system performance, and maintain system security through proper user and permission management. Each chapter has provided you with practical skills that you can use in everyday situations, increasing your confidence in managing and troubleshooting Linux systems.

The learning doesn't end here. The abilities and knowledge you've learned serve as a starting point for more advanced expertise. To become a truly skilled and diverse system administrator, you must constantly increase your skill set and knowledge base. For individuals who want to go deeper into the complexities of Linux system administration, we are glad to introduce the accompanying book, "Linux Advanced for SysAdmin."

"Linux Advanced for SysAdmin" advances your knowledge by focusing on advanced topics including security configuration, network management, and large-scale system monitoring. You'll learn how to manage databases, do advanced system monitoring, and handle complex tasks like Kubernetes, load balancing, and deployments. This advanced guide is intended to supplement the fundamental information you have received in this book, giving you with the expertise required to tackle complex and challenging jobs in Linux system administration.

By reading both "Linux Basics for SysAdmin" and "Linux Advanced for SysAdmin," you will be well-prepared to manage a variety of administrative jobs, making you a great asset to any IT team. Together, these publications provide a thorough guide to becoming a skilled, effective, and adaptable Linux system administrator. There are limitless opportunities waiting for you in the IT field if you accept Linux, keep learning, and maintain a curious mind.

Thank You

www.ingramcontent.com/pod-product-compliance
Lightning Source LLC
Chambersburg PA
CBHW080211170726
48282CB00030B/1081
9788119177561